ANTAR

Guide to your adventure

Jacquetta Megarry

Rucksack Readers

ANTARCTICA *Guide to your adventure*

First published 2024 by
Rucksack Readers, 6 Old Church Lane, Edinburgh, EH15 3PX, UK

Phone   0131 661 0262 (+44 131 661 0262)
Email: **info@rucsacs.com**
Website   *www.rucsacs.com*

978-1-913817-08-4

British Library cataloguing in publication data: a catalogue record for this book is available from the British Library.

Design and illustrations by Ian Clydesdale: ian@clydesdale.scot

Printed on snowproof, biodegradable paper in the Czech Republic via Akcent Media of St Neots, UK

The mapping on pages 7, 9 and 67 is © Maps International 2019 and is based on their excellent large wall map of Antarctica *bit.ly/MI-ant* which we highly recommend. It includes bathymetry data supplied by the British Oceanographic Data Centre, and data derived from the Antarctic Digital Database (version 4·0) © Scientific Committee on Antarctic Research Cambridge 2002. All other maps are © Rucksack Readers 2024.

Biosecurity 2023-24, IAATO and updates

In October 2023, IAATO announced enhanced biosecurity measures to avoid pathogenic avian flu spreading to Antarctica. These prohibited contact with the ground with anything other than your rubber boots, and, if approached by wildlife, required you to back off to maintain a 5-metre distance. Nobody knows how long these rules will be needed, or whether stricter ones may be imposed. They were not in force when the photos in this book were taken and may restrict specialist activities that are mentioned. Always follow the current rules as advised by your IAATO tour operator; visit the IAATO website for any updates and watch its short video of Visitor Guidelines: *www.iaato.org*

All information was checked prior to publication. However, changes are inevitable: check carefully with your agent before booking any trip and expect to sign a disclaimer: the Antarctic environment is inhospitable, unpredictable and potentially dangerous. You are responsible for your own safety and welfare while abroad.

We may post important updates on the book's own page: *www.rucsacs.com/books/aga*. We welcome comments and suggestions from readers. All feedback will be followed up, and readers whose comments lead to changes will be entitled to claim a free copy of any book from our website *www.rucsacs.com*. Please email comments to **info@rucsacs.com**.

Foreword

I first tried to to get to the frozen continent back in the 1970s, applying repeatedly for jobs with the British Antarctic Survey. Alas, they always turned me down. When eventually I did get to go there, it was as co-leader of a private expedition to South Georgia in 1989. I have now made 14 trips to that mountainous island and to the Antarctic Peninsula, and the dazzling combination of ocean, mountains, ice and teeming wildlife remains as enchanting as ever.

Jacquetta Megarry clearly shares that sense of enchantment. More to the point, she has packed this excellent guide with sound practical advice and a wealth of fascinating information on the science and history of the world's highest, driest, coldest continent. I never knew, for instance, how much of Antarctica's landmass lies beneath sea level. This guide makes a perfect introduction to the journey of a lifetime.

Stephen Venables
stephenvenables.org

Introduction to Antarctica

Antarctica is the most extreme of all continents. As Venables remarks, it is the highest, driest and coldest continent, and it is also by far the windiest: speeds of up to 199 mph (321 kph) have been recorded. First sighted in 1820, it has no permanent human population. Its 74 research stations host about 1100 people in winter and 5000 in summer, but all are temporary.

Over 98% of its surface is covered in ice, with an average depth of 1·2 miles (1·9 km). With hardly any vegetation, it has no land-based animal life. However, wildlife is abundant in the surrounding seas and in the air above. Antarctica is very different from the Arctic – an ocean surrounded by land masses. Instead, it is a huge, high land mass surrounded by nutrient-rich oceans: see the images on page 6. Beneath its massive ice sheet lies a mountainous, largely unknown land.

Antarctica is a continent, but not a country. It has no sovereign government and no permanent residents. It is one of the few places in the world where there has never been war, where the environment is protected with stringent regulations and biosecurity measures, and where scientific research takes priority. There is no room for complacency that this will endure, and some challenges remain: see page 84.

Arctic Circle   *Antarctic Circle*

Following the International Geophysical Year 1957-58, the 12 countries then active in the continent signed the Antarctic Treaty in Washington in 1959. This asserts freedom of scientific investigation and cooperation and bans military activity. It did not resolve territorial claims, but effectively set them aside by 'freezing' them. The treaty is due to be reviewed in 2048, and is discussed further, along with the Madrid Protocol, on page 83.

Visitor numbers have increased rapidly in recent years: in the 2002-3 season there were about 25,000, but by 2019-20 the number had more than doubled to 56,000. In 2022-3 visitor numbers reached about 78,000 and by 2023-4 over 100,000. The time may be approaching when further restrictions are needed to protect the world's only pristine continent.

This book is for anybody who is thinking of visiting Antarctica. We offer advice about how to choose your trip and information that may help you to make the most of it. Aim to read at least Part 1 before you book a trip, and Part 4 long before you leave. Dip into Part 5 to decide on further reading and web browsing. Parts 2 and 3 are suitable both as onboard reading and before departure. Our overall goal is to inspire interest in this outstanding continent while encouraging responsible, informed and sustainable tourism.

Size and location

It is difficult to grasp the sheer scale of Antarctica. Over 75% larger than the contiguous United States (see opposite), it is nearly twice the area of Australia. Surprisingly, it is a more extreme desert, with precipitation (rain and/or snow) only one quarter that of Australia. Your mental image of Antarctica may feature snow and ice, but very little moisture falls from the sky. Howling winds can whip up loose snow and ice, and blizzards are common. The Antarctic air is so cold that it can hold very little moisture. Strong air currents circulate around the pole, isolating its generally high-pressure weather from the lower pressure systems at lower latitudes.

The continent's extent is much greater in winter than in summer. So much sea ice forms that its area can apparently double in size. Since ice forms and melts each year, geographers take the continent's true limit to be the *Antarctic Convergence*. This irregular boundary marks the junction between very cold, Antarctic north-flowing water and the warmer sub-Antarctic seas. When on board ship you may even notice it as an abrupt drop in air temperature. The Convergence hovers around a latitude of 60° S and its position varies seasonally and over the years.

Antarctica is much further away than most people imagine: the very shortest journey is from Ushuaia, at the southern tip of South America, to the northern tip of the Antarctic Peninsula. Even that is some 620 miles/1000 km across the notorious Drake Passage: see page 9. Journeys from New Zealand are much longer, about 3100 miles/4990 km as the plane flies. The only time when cruise ships visit is the Antarctic summer: between April and September, the only winter visitors are teams of scientists and support staff based on the research stations.

Because of the immense distances and the desire to make time for landings once Antarctica is reached, most cruises explore only the northern tip of its Peninsula. The great majority never even cross the Antarctic Circle (66° 34′S) although many will approach it to within a degree or two; each degree of latitude equates to about 69 miles/111 km. The map below focuses on the most visited area, together with the South Shetland Islands where ships tend to land before crossing the Bransfield Strait. Two aspects of the map to note are its very small scale, and that the area shown as 'land' varies greatly through the seasons as the pack ice advances and retreats.

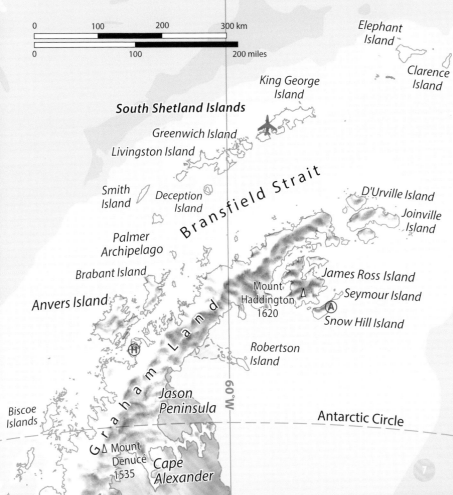

If crossing the Circle is your priority, be aware that this will determine which month you can visit because of pack ice. It may also affect your choice of ship, depending on its rating for ice-breaking: see page 28. It will result in an itinerary with many more long days at sea and fewer landings than otherwise. Even those cruises that habitually cross the Circle are sometimes defeated by bad weather or unexpected pack ice.

Pack ice grows over the winter months, achieving its maximum area in September. In 2023, NASA reported the extent of the pack ice was the smallest ever recorded: 17 million sq km (6·6 million sq miles) marks a decline of nearly 10% compared with the 1981-2010 median area, shown by the yellow dotted line above. This is probably a by-product of global warming. In any ambitious itinerary, remember that the extent of the pack ice varies greatly from year to year. For a website with a brilliant video animation of the process, see page 95.

In general, any Antarctic itinerary is a statement of intent, not a binding contract; the weather, sea state and pack ice determine where each ship can visit safely.

Myths about daylight

There are widespread myths about the daylight in Antarctica. Three factors determine the hours of lightness and darkness anywhere on earth, at sea level:
• **latitude**   • **season**   • **environmental**.

On a standard Antarctic cruise you may never cross the Antarctic Circle, currently 66° 34' south of the equator: its exact position varies very slowly with fractional changes in the tilt of the earth's axis – only by up to 2° over 41,000 years. Outside the Antarctic Circle, you will never see the sun above the horizon at midnight, though you may experience a surprising level of light at twilight: see below and page 10.

If experiencing midnight sun – or mid-day darkness – is your goal, it's much easier to go to Tromsø, Norway at latitude 69° 39' N – a beautiful, inhabited city that is easily accessible, with airport, universities and hospitals. The northern hemisphere of our planet is hospitable to humans up to far higher latitudes than is the southern.

Midnight sun over the Antarctic coastline

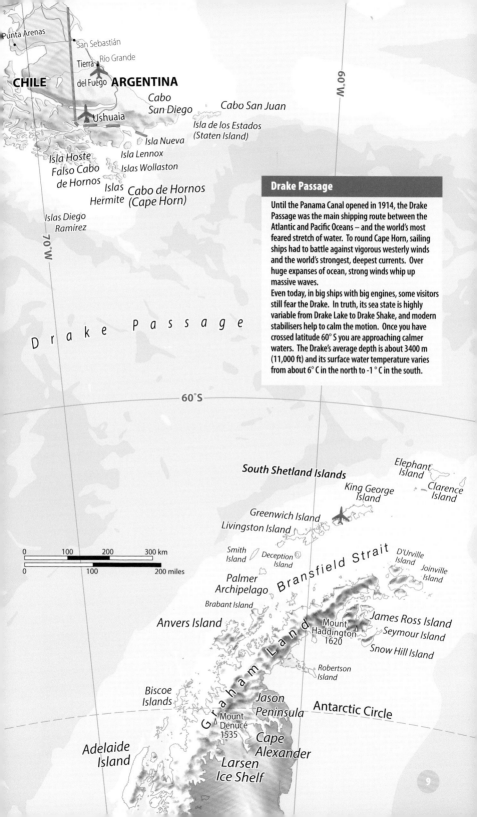

Punta Arenas

San Sebastián

Río Grande

Tierra del Fuego

CHILE

ARGENTINA

Ushuaia

Cabo San Diego

Cabo San Juan

Isla de los Estados (Staten Island)

Isla Nueva

Isla Hoste

Isla Lennox

Falso Cabo de Hornos

Islas Wollaston

Islas Hermite

Cabo de Hornos (Cape Horn)

Islas Diego Ramírez

70° W.

60° W.

D r a k e   P a s s a g e

Drake Passage

Until the Panama Canal opened in 1914, the Drake Passage was the main shipping route between the Atlantic and Pacific Oceans – and the world's most feared stretch of water. To round Cape Horn, sailing ships had to battle against vigorous westerly winds and the world's strongest, deepest currents. Over huge expanses of ocean, strong winds whip up massive waves.

Even today, in big ships with big engines, some visitors still fear the Drake. In truth, its sea state is highly variable from Drake Lake to Drake Shake, and modern stabilisers help to calm the motion. Once you have crossed latitude 60° S you are approaching calmer waters. The Drake's average depth is about 3400 m (11,000 ft) and its surface water temperature varies from about 6° C in the north to -1 ° C in the south.

60° S

South Shetland Islands

Elephant Island

Clarence Island

King George Island

Greenwich Island

Livingston Island

| 0 | 100 | 200 | 300 km |
| 0 | 100 | | 200 miles |

Smith Island

Deception Island

D'Urville Island

Joinville Island

Br a n s f i e l d   S t r a i t

Palmer Archipelago

Brabant Island

Anvers Island

Mount Haddington 1620

James Ross Island

Seymour Island

Snow Hill Island

Robertson Island

Biscoe Islands

Jason Peninsula

G r a h a m   L a n d

Mount Denucé 1535

Cape Alexander

Antarctic Circle

Adelaide Island

Larsen Ice Shelf

9

McMurdo Station, latitude nearly 78° S

The second factor is season. Unless you are employed in the military or on a research station, you won't be visiting Antarctica in winter. Antarctic summer officially lasts from late September to late March. At the South Pole, 24-hour daylight lasts from 21/22 September to 21/22 March.

However, most visitors set off between November and February and reach their 'farthest south' in the middle of their trips. The Antarctic summer solstice is usually 21 December and on that day the sun will be above the horizon for 24 hours only inside the Antarctic Circle. Rothera, the British research station on Adelaide Island is at latitude 67° 34' S so it's only just inside the Circle. Even so, it has continuous daylight of some kind for up to six weeks from early December to late January. As a rule of thumb, the number of days of continuous daylight or darkness increases by about six days per degree of latitude.

Data on daylight is theoretical, calculated from astrophysics and calendars. In the real world, refraction causes bending of light that originates below the horizon. Also, reflection from white surfaces such as snow and ice amplifies the ambient light. Your brain's threshold for detecting light may be lower than usual because of the absence of light pollution and the long, slow Antarctic decline in illumination. So your ability to see may persist long after your camera ceases to register any ambient light.

Even when below the horizon, the sun's light creates various degrees of twilight – known as civil, nautical or astronomical, depending on whether the sun's midpoint is 6°, 12° or 18° below the horizon. In winter, twilight-free darkness occurs only at latitudes higher than 88° 33' i.e. places that no ordinary visitor will ever reach. Even so, the extreme blackness of the Antarctic polar night lasts for about 11 weeks, not six months. And anyway local factors, including height above sea level, mean that generally it seems lighter than you expect, even when the sun is technically below the horizon.

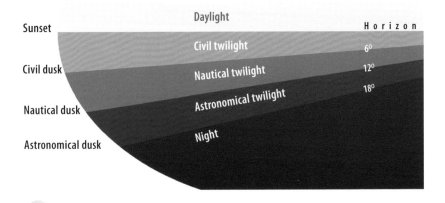

1 Briefing before you go

Before you book

An early question is whether you are going alone, or with a partner or friend(s)? Very few ships offer dedicated single cabins, and the supplement for sole occupancy of a double cabin is typically 70%. However some companies waive the single supplement on certain departure dates and itineraries, and others offer widespread waivers or reductions as a marketing tool. Since trips to Antarctica are expensive even without a supplement, for many solo travellers the size (or avoidance) of the single supplement may be a decisive factor, occasionally overtaken by other discounts and deals.

Socially there is no problem about going solo: your fellow passengers share your interest in Antarctica and its wildlife; making friends is easy in an informal atmosphere. And a surprising number of solo travellers turn out not to be single, but have partners back home who couldn't, or didn't want to, visit Antarctica.

The pros and cons of when you travel include price, climate, daylight and the stages in the breeding or migration cycles of whichever wildlife interests you most. Which species do you most want to see, which parts of Antarctica are you keen to reach and do you care about being awake for sunrise and/or sunset? Read Part 2 to understand the timing of penguin breeding. Do you want to see adults mating, nest-building or eggs hatching, or are you hoping for cute downy penguin chicks or juveniles? For whales, be aware of their migration patterns and the timing of their journeys.

Departures before mid-November and in March are considered early or late season, with December/January as high season and everything in between as shoulder season. No visitors travel between April and September because it is Antarctic winter.

Book early for maximum choice. Check that the operator is a member of the International Association of Antarctic Tour Operators (IAATO). It was founded in 1991 to promote safe and responsible Antarctic travel: look for its logo and see pages 83-4. Ensure that you have generous cancellation insurance in place before committing yourself even to a deposit.

Juvenile King penguins, South Georgia, late November

How cold will it be?

Antarctica has three main climatic regions: the Peninsula, the coastal region and the interior – mainly high plateau. The interior is *much* colder with barely any snowfall, but visitors don't go there so we exclude it here. Instead we focus on two Antarctic stations, plus South Georgia to represent the much-visited sub-Antarctic islands. They have milder, wetter climates.

The map shows locations for the three weather stations – Grytviken (54° 17′ S) for South Georgia, Rothera (67° 34′ S) to indicate the Antarctic Peninsula and McMurdo (77° 50′ S) for the continent's low-lying coastal margins.

Don't be over-influenced by the climate statistics: the wind, weather and your likely activities on the day are a better guide to how cold you will feel, what clothing you need and what precautions you should take. Read on about wind chill, and also about specialist activities. A Zodiac cruise is a different experience in sunny, calm conditions (see the photo below) from the same trip in high winds.

The charts opposite present month-by-month data for all three stations. South Georgia has a relatively temperate climate, at least at sea level. Its latitude is equivalent to halfway between London and Edinburgh, but the chilling effect of its high mountains and exposed location makes its climate much colder. August is its coldest month, with temperatures dipping to -2 °C and rising to only 5 °C, whilst in summer months the maximum daytime temperature hovers in the range 8-11 °C.

Rothera, just inside the Antarctic Circle, is much colder in winter with a mean daily range of -14 °C to -6 °C. However, in the summer months when you are likely to visit, it's only about 5 °C cooler than South Georgia. The seasonal range is much wider for McMurdo, where winter daily temperatures plunge to -32 °C at night, and fail to rise above -23 °C in the daytime. Again, the summer months have a narrower gap between daily minimum and maximum, but are still about 5 °C lower than Rothera and 10 °C lower than South Georgia.

A Zodiac cruise around Cuverville Island

Turning to precipitation (snow, hail, sleet and rain), the contrasts are so strong that the bar charts below had to be drawn at different scales. The annual totals are drastically different: South Georgia had a mean annual total of 1400 mm (55 in), whereas Rothera received only half that (710 mm/28 in) and McMurdo less than 10% (112 mm/4 in). In Antarctica, more precipitation falls in winter months than in summer, a trend that is less marked for South Georgia. For comparison, over the same period London had an annual total of 610 mm (24 in), whilst New York had about 1140 mm (45 in) – in both cases distributed more evenly across the months.

Temperature and precipitation data for three weather stations, 2005-2015

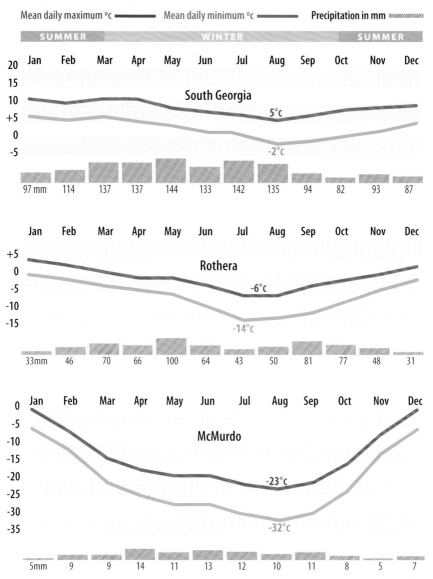

Mean daily maximum °c ——— Mean daily minimum °c ——— Precipitation in mm ////////

| SUMMER | WINTER | SUMMER |

South Georgia

97 mm · 114 · 137 · 137 · 144 · 133 · 142 · 135 · 94 · 82 · 93 · 87

5°c
-2°c

Rothera

33mm · 46 · 70 · 66 · 100 · 64 · 43 · 50 · 81 · 77 · 48 · 31

-6°c
-14°c

McMurdo

5mm · 9 · 9 · 14 · 11 · 13 · 12 · 10 · 11 · 8 · 5 · 7

-23°c
-32°c

High winds create rough seas off the South Shetlands

Famously the windiest of all continents, Antarctica's massive high, cold plateau can lead to *katabatic* winds of enormous speeds. Gravity draws the heavier cold air northward down from the central plateau, sometimes at terrifying speed. In Terre-Adélie, speeds of 125 mph/200 kph have occurred over 50 times since 1956 and a record of 199 mph (321 kph) was captured in 1972. Walking against a wind of 95 mph/155 kph is physically impossible: even strong, heavy humans resort to crawling on hands and knees.

The coastal regions and Peninsula are generally less windy than the interior of the continent. Wind chill is as important as air temperature in determining how cold you will feel. When in Antarctica, before deciding what to wear, don't ask about the temperature: ask instead about the wind speeds expected – and remember that a ride in a Zodiac brings extra wind chill all of its own.

The table below shows combinations of wind and temperature that will create frostbite in exposed flesh within 30, 10 and 5 minutes colour-coded from mid-blue to purple. It shows that (for example) a wind speed of 50 kph (31 mph) makes a temperature of -25 °C feel like -42 °C and you can expect frostbite within five to ten minutes. In a strong wind (100 kph/62 mph) it will feel like -47 °C and frostbite will occur in under five minutes.

Wind chill increases the risk of frostbite

		temperature °C								
wind speed (km/hr)	0	0	-5	-10	-15	-20	-25	-30	-35	0
	10	-3	-9	-15	-21	-27	-33	-39	-45	10
	20	-5	-12	-18	-24	-31	-37	-43	-49	
	30	-7	-13	-20	-26	-33	-39	-46	-52	20
	40	-7	-14	-21	-27	-34	-41	-48	-54	
	50	-8	-15	-22	-29	-35	-42	-49	-56	30
	60	-9	-16	-23	-30	-37	-43	-50	-57	40
	70	-9	-16	-23	-30	-37	-44	-51	-59	
	80	-10	-17	-24	-31	-38	-45	-52	-60	50
	90	-10	-17	-25	-32	-39	-46	-53	-61	60
	100	-11	-18	-25	-32	-40	-47	-54	-61	

30 mins · 10 mins · 5 mins

wind speed (mph)

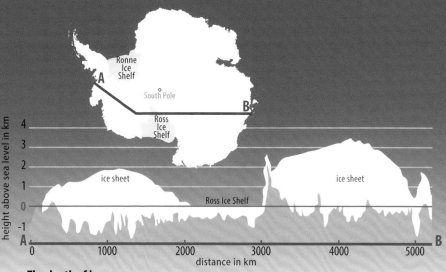

The depth of ice

The world's highest continent has an average elevation of 2300 m (7500 ft). These great altitudes are achieved by its thick covering of ice, with only 2% of the land area ice-free. No two-dimensional map can convey how much ice there is, because its depth varies so much. It isn't spread out in a thin layer like a shallow lake, but a vast body of ice with deep abysses and shallows like the ocean. Think of it as an immense, dense blanket draped over the high plateau, flowing very slowly downhill, filling all the valleys and entirely burying most of the high mountains.

The diagram above shows a transect of Antarctica from A, near the base of its Peninsula going towards and across the Ross Ice Shelf, to reach the ocean at B. It shows how much the depth of the ice cover varies across the continent. Beyond the Transantarctic mountains lies the massive high plateau of East Antarctica. The continent's thickest ice (not on this transect) extends up to 4·8 km/3 miles deep.

The diagram also shows that a large amount of the ice sheet (over 40% by area) is resting on bedrock that is *below* the current sea level (the dark blue line). That means that warming ocean water could melt its way in and will seep under the ice under the influence of gravity. The danger of melting ice from the bottom upwards is insidious. The warming ocean is a greater threat to Antarctic ice than is a warming atmosphere.

Midnight light over the pack ice, Ross Sea

When to go, and what it costs

The full season runs from late October to March: only a small number of committed professionals work through the Antarctic winter. In general, high season is the most expensive (December and January), whereas the shoulder season (November and February) will cost less. Although bargain or special-purpose trips may be offered from late October or into early March, early and late season dates carry higher risks that weather and pack ice will disrupt plans, so are less likely to appeal to first-timers.

So what are the factors, month by month? November is best for an experience of pristine wilderness, with icebergs at their largest, landing sites snowy rather than muddy and penguins likely to be mating, nest-building and laying. For photographers, the chance of glorious sunrises and sunsets may be important, before too much daylight starts to encroach at both ends of a short – perhaps very short – night. By December, you are unlikely to be awake around dusk or dawn, and extremely unlikely to experience both if you need anything like normal hours of sleep. So November may actually seem preferable to the long daylight of late December. This is Antarctic spring, so the weather is less predictable, and some sites may not yet be accessible because of pack ice. The range of wildlife that you see may be restricted to adult penguins and seabirds, unless you are lucky enough to be seeking Emperor penguins.

December and January bring warmer weather, even longer daylight and a wider range of wildlife. You may see penguin chicks hatching and seal pups birthing. However the popularity of these months make them busier, and you may have to book further in

Mt Scott (left) seen from the Lemaire Channel, near Booth Island

advance and pay more. High season is great for long, light days – but don't expect to see the midnight sun unless your itinerary has been planned to cross the Antarctic Circle. However, once some ice has melted the chances of landing on remote sites improve.

Late season is the best option if you hope to cross the Antarctic Circle, and (like early season) you can enjoy the pleasures of both sunrise and sunset over the wild scenery. You are also more likely to see whales in February, although some species have started migrating by then. By March the pack ice is forming, the days are getting shorter and most species will have left the land for sea. However the timing varies widely from year to year, and modern ice-strengthened ships (see page 56) may schedule departures throughout March. For some, the chance of a bargain by travelling off-season or at short notice may compensate for any risks.

Gentoo penguin chick soliciting food from its parent

Zodiacs ferry passengers from ship to shore

What is included?

Before choosing among options, it is important to compare like with like. Most operators market cruises to clients in many countries, so prices seldom include flights from your home country. However many include the Buenos Aires/Ushuaia or Santiago de Chile/Ushuaia return flight, and some also a pre-cruise night in a hotel and possibly even a night in Ushuaia. This became more common when Antarctica trips resumed post-pandemic, partly because the operators wanted to keep the ship's group together and to organise timely Covid testing.

Packages include meals, snacks and soft drinks on board, excursions on Zodiacs and all regular landings. They also include the use of the ship's rubber boots throughout the trip. Don't even consider taking your own boots: you wouldn't be allowed to use them because of biosecurity: see page 31. If your feet are unusually large or small, it makes sense to notify your size in advance. If the activities includes snowshoeing then check if they are offered free or for hire. Many ships also supply a branded waterproof jacket (parka) which may be warmly lined or merely waterproof: find out which, because you need to take clothes that can comfortably be layered, see page 87.

Aside from footwear/jackets, there's a range of other possible extras such as internet access, alcoholic drinks and room service. Generally, the more expensive packages are more likely to include any or all of these extras, but premium drinks, spa treatments and laundry will normally be charged extra. Internet access involves satellite connections, so the bandwidth can be very limited and anything more than basic emailing can prove quite expensive. Even if it's included, expect usage restrictions.

Specialist activities range enormously in their costs and availability: see page 30. It would be easy to spend hundreds, possibly thousands, of dollars on onboard extras, and some packages include an amount of onboard spend with the cruise. A particular issue is that of tipping, which is generally paid into a pooled fund so that crew who are not customer-facing don't get left out.

Recommended tipping rates vary widely, but about USD15 per passenger per day on board was not uncommon in 2023-24; expectations can only rise with inflation. To ensure that tips reach the intended destination, cash may be preferable. Whilst tipping is in theory optional, when you see how hard everybody works to make the most of the opportunities, you may feel churlish if not ready to tip appropriately. To complicate matters, a few cruises state that tipping is included.

Where to go, and for how long?

Most first-timers are aiming at the least inaccessible parts of Antarctica. For them, the choice is whether to focus on the Antarctic Peninsula itself – with visits en route to the South Shetlands – or whether to include either or both of the British Overseas Territories of South Georgia and the Falklands. Also known as sub-Antarctic islands, there are strong reasons to consider visiting either – or both. The downside is that each destination adds to the length and cost of your trip, and adds to the number of days spent wholly at sea. Refer to page 25 for an idea of the distances involved.

Another perspective is that if you plan to endure an epic journey to reach this part of the world, and might never return, you would miss too much if you don't visit South Georgia and/or the Falklands. Your journey to Ushuaia is likely to take longer than you may imagine because any series of flights will need some safety margins for connections, and may involve some overnights en route and/or on planes, especially on the outward journey to avoid the risk of missing your cruise departure.

Unless you are lucky enough to live near a suitable hub airport in the Americas, you may find that any Antarctic trip requires an extra overhead of 3-4 days of travel or stopover. This may tempt you to book a shorter trip on the cruise ship. And if you are determined to spend as long as possible in Antarctica itself, or keen to cross the Antarctic Circle, then for any given budget be aware that that time spent in the sub-Antarctic islands will be at the price of days on Antarctica itself.

For the minority with plenty of time and money, especially if focused on the history of its exploration, the goal may be the Ross Sea and Ice Shelf, a remote area more easily reached from New Zealand than from South America. This is where the early explorers gained a toehold for exploring the interior, with the Ross Ice Shelf offering the shortest distance to the South Pole. Here you can visit the timber huts left by Robert Scott and Ernest Shackleton: see page 65 and the map on page 67.

Ross Island is home to two research stations: New Zealand's modest Scott Base and the US's massive McMurdo Station. The latter's facilities include the Chapel of the Snows, hospital, hydroponic greenhouse, newspaper and media, fire department, diving recompression chamber and fuel-tank farm. The volcano Mt Erebus towers over the landscape and the terrain of the Dry Valleys closely resembles that of Mars. But this area is far removed from typical itineraries of cruises and further detail lies outside the scope of this book.

Helicopter landing on the slopes of Mt Erebus

The Falklands

The Falklands archipelago comprises over 700 islands, most of them small and uninhabited, with some wonderful wildlife viewing as well as human interest of various kinds. The two main islands are divided by a deep channel, the Falkland Sound, and they are in marked contrast. Most of the population of 3200 live on East Falkland, which has many small settlements linked by roads, Mount Pleasant airport and the capital Stanley. Its latitude (51° 42′ S) mirrors that of London (51° 31′ N) almost exactly.

Stanley became the capital only in 1845, and was a major port in the 19th century for ships needing repair after rounding Cape Horn. Ship repairs soon started to decline, and were finished off by the Panama Canal opening in 1914. However Stanley remained an important base for sealing and whaling ships. The Maritime History Trail features a number of historic shipwrecks around its harbour. More recently, the islands were the location of the Argentinian invasion of Las Malvinas in 1982 which led to an 11-week war with Britain. For some visitors, this lends a key historical interest to any visit and suggests itineraries that include East Falkland.

Many cruise ships, but not all, visit Stanley at the eastern edge of East Falkland. Despite its city status (awarded in 2022), its population is only about 2500 – nearly 80% that of the whole territory. Its older parts are made colourful by brightly painted buildings,

flowery gardens and patriotic flags. Its attractions include the Falkland Islands Museum, Government House (built in 1845), the town hall, several war memorials, a 1933 whalebone arch and three churches – including Christ Church, the world's southernmost Anglican cathedral: see the photo below. An annual ceremony takes place at the 1982 War Memorial on 14 June. Leisure facilities include a racecourse, swimming pool and golf course. Some visitors find the old-fashioned pubs, speech and clothing of the residents intriguing, akin to a time-warped English village.

West Falkland is very sparsely populated, and generally more mountainous – albeit East Falkland has the Wickham Heights with Mount Usborne. The West has an extravagantly serrated coastline with many fjords, cliffs and inlets. Its offshore islands are important breeding grounds for seabirds and penguins.

Beyond West Falkland lies New Island, some 150 miles west of Stanley, with good natural harbours used long ago by sealers and whalers. Five whalers were stranded here in 1813 and the hut that they built for shelter has been restored as a museum. The island is now privately owned and hosts two nature reserves with 41 species of breeding birds and regular sightings of Peale's dolphins. Four species of penguin (Gentoo, Rockhopper, King and Magellanic) flourish side by side and there are Black-browed albatrosses, petrels, caracaras (both striated and crested) and Fur seals. For more about these species, see pages 36 to 45.

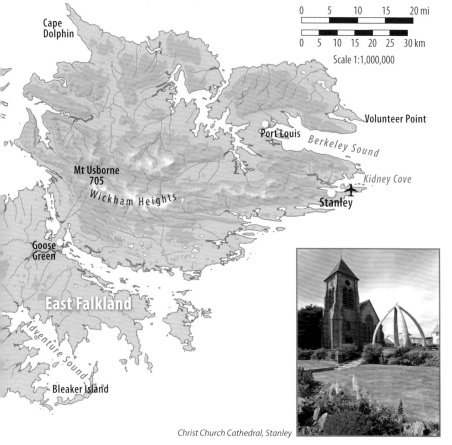

| 0 | 5 | 10 | 15 | 20 mi |

| 0 | 5 | 10 | 15 | 20 | 25 | 30 km |

Scale 1:1,000,000

Cape Dolphin

Volunteer Point

Port Louis

Berkeley Sound

Mt Usborne 705

Kidney Cove

Wickham Heights

Stanley

Goose Green

East Falkland

Adventure Sound

Bleaker Island

Christ Church Cathedral, Stanley

Sea Lion Island

South Georgia

South Georgia appeals to visitors for two main reasons: it hosts immense populations of wildlife which have been protected for long enough to be surprisingly relaxed around visitors, and its human history is fascinating, with the dark days of sealing and whaling followed by an extraordinary biological renaissance. Like the Falklands, South Georgia is a British Overseas Territory – officially known as South Georgia and the South Sandwich Islands, the latter being a chain of much smaller islands lying 450 miles/725 km to its south-east.

Bird Island

Bay of Isles

King Haakon Bay

Nobody lives on South Georgia permanently, although about 30-40 people live there at any one time, most of them doing scientific research. In summer, a few people staff the island's museum at Grytviken: visit it online at *sgmuseum.gs* or in person if you land there. It lies at the head of King Edward Cove, the best anchorage in South Georgia, and the museum is on the site of the Villa, the whaling station manager's house which burned down in 1914. The replacement building remained the centre of management at Grytviken until whaling ceased after 60 years, in 1964. The building lay empty for nearly 30 years, but then after restoration it opened to visitors as a museum in 1992. The nearby Norwegian-style Lutheran Whalers' Church was built in 1913: see the photo opposite.

Most of the island is covered in ice and snow for most of the year, and the terrain is steep and rocky, with prominent mountains and glaciers that tumble down into the sea. The Allardyce and Salvesen ranges form the spine of the island, rising to Mount Paget (2935 m/9630 ft) – first climbed in December 1964 by a British military team. Glaciers and steep mountain slopes create a formidable barrier between its two main coasts, as Shackleton and his companions found to their cost: see page 78. There is little vegetation, mostly grasses and mosses, and hardly any potentially arable land – quite a contrast with the Falklands.

The south-west coast is very exposed to the westerly weather and waves, and King Haakon Bay gave little protection to Shackleton's *James Caird* when it landed there in May 1916. All the whaling stations had been built on the sheltered bays of the north-east coast. The story of how he, Worsley and Crean managed to cross South Georgia to raise rescue from Stromness is told on pages 74-9.

Memorials at Grytviken

The graveyard has 63 gravestones oriented east-west as is traditional, and only one loner that points south. Shackleton was buried here on 5 March 1922, see page 80, and his grave evokes the title of his famous book. For the extraordinary discovery made exactly 100 years after his burial, see page 82.

To the right is a memorial stone to Frank Wild, whose ashes were brought here in 2011. A ceremony was held in the Whaler's Church, attended by Wild and Shackleton descendants. The church also has a memorial stone to Tom Crean and to the station's founder, Anton Larsen.

First visited by Captain Cook in 1775, South Georgia quickly became known for its abundant population of Elephant and Fur seals. The story of the industrial levels of hunting to near-extinction, first of seals, then whales, is told on pages 62-3. To help modern visitors to learn about this history of exploitation, the South Georgia Heritage Trust invested £7.5 million in conserving Grytviken whaling station, the only one that you can visit. It had to make the buildings safe and carried out an extensive environmental cleanup in 2003-5. They also installed information boards that explain how the whalers lived, ate and worked.

The main hazard for modern visitors is to remain alert to, and maintain a suitable distance from, the large numbers of penguins and seals that understandably regard Grytviken as their own territory. When I visited, King penguins were everywhere and seem untroubled by humans, indeed often quite curious. Fur seals were resting, some nursing their pups (this was February) and it was fascinating to watch them chasing off the South Georgia pintail ducks. For the story of how this and other endemic species were rescued from the edge of extinction, see page 32.

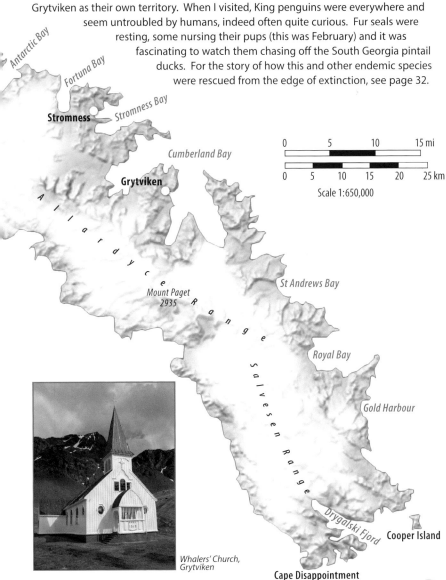

Antarctic Bay

Fortuna Bay

Stromness — Stromness Bay

Cumberland Bay

Grytviken

A l l a r d y c e

Mount Paget
2935

R a n g e

St Andrews Bay

Royal Bay

S a l v e s e n   R a n g e

Gold Harbour

Drygalski Fjord   Cooper Island

Cape Disappointment

Whalers' Church,
Grytviken

0   5   10   15 mi

0   5   10   15   20   25 km

Scale 1:650,000

The abundance of wildlife on South Georgia makes a number of locations very popular for landings. Gold Harbour has some 30,000 breeding pairs of King penguins, often mixed with hundreds of Gentoos. Look out for Antarctic terns, Southern giant petrels and Light-mantled sooty albatrosses. Further north-west, St Andrews Bay hosts the island's largest colony of King penguins, probably the largest in the world. Estimates vary from 150,000 to 250,000 breeding pairs, with an apparently steady rise in the numbers and the great difficulty of making a precise count obvious. The sight, sound and smell of up to half a million King penguins is unforgettable: I will take it to my grave.

King penguin colony, St Andrews Bay, South Georgia

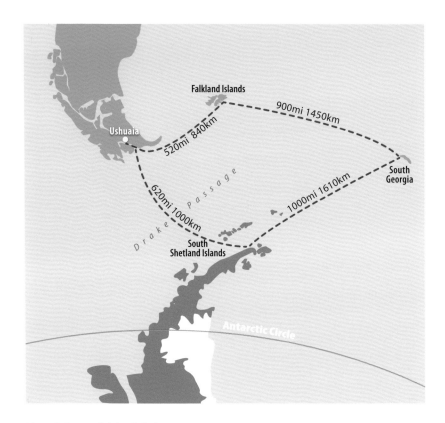

Falkland Islands

900mi 1450km

Ushuaia

520mi 840km

South
Georgia

620mi 1000km

Drake Passage

1000mi 1610km

South
Shetland Islands

Antarctic Circle

The sub-Antarctic island choice

Take a close look at the detailed itineraries on offer, and you'll find that most visit both or neither of the sub-Antarctic islands. So if you have a strong preference to visit one but not the other, you need to filter the options on this criterion first. Traditionally the pattern was to proceed clockwise – Ushuaia, Falklands, South Georgia, Antarctica, Ushuaia – but at least during the season 2021/22 this pattern was reversed. The reason was Covid-related: the Falklands government was insisting on ships being Covid-free for five days before arrival, and since it takes only two days of sailing from Ushuaia this dictated the anticlockwise direction.

This is a huge circuit that demands many days at sea. You are travelling well over 3000 miles/4830 km before you do any cruising around any of the destinations. If your priority is to spend time on Antarctica itself, you face some difficult decisions about whether to include either or both sub-Antarctic islands.

Where to start from

Aside from a small minority of ships that sail from Australia or New Zealand, usually heading for the Ross Sea area, nearly all departures are from Argentina or Chile. About 90% of all visitors leave from Ushuaia (Argentina) because of its favourable location for the Drake Passage, but the Punta Arenas (Chile) option may appeal if you are keen to voyage around the legendary Cape Horn, if you want to combine your trip with cruising coastal Patagonia, or if you want to fly across the Drake.

Some people are so concerned about seasickness in the Drake Passage that they prefer to fly it in at least one direction. The flight leaves from Punta Arenas, Chile and lands on King George Island – the largest of the South Shetlands. It takes only about two hours, compared with two days on a ship. However, that assumes that your plane can take off as planned: planes are much more vulnerable than ships to poor visibility, high winds and excessive ice and snow. For a flight to work, conditions must be safe for landing, as well as for take-off.

Therefore fly-cruise expeditions have to build some flexibility into their itineraries, with a few days of buffer activity in case of flight disruption. Before committing yourself to the flight option, it's worth considering how you will feel about these buffer days. You will also find that you face a very limited choice of cruise departures from King George Island, so choosing to fly may also dictate the size of vessel, level of comfort and date of your departure, as well as obviously increasing its cost. As an aside, Antarctic sightseeing flights were discontinued after the 1979 crash by an Air New Zealand plane in which 257 people died. For more about motion sickness, see pages 90-92.

Whatever itinerary you decide upon, remember that each Antarctic itinerary is an expression of intent, not a contract. Conditions – especially wind, sea state and pack ice – determine where cruises can go and whether landings are possible. The ship's captain may be obliged to vary the itinerary in the interests of safety.

Bootwash before boarding the plane at King George Island

How to choose your ship

Le Boréal, a modern all-balcony ship

The most important aspect of an Antarctic ship is its size: specifically, what maximum number has been set for passengers? Labels may differ, but a vessel that can take 201-500 passengers is normally regarded as a cruise ship and has some serious limitations over landings. In particular, the Antarctic Treaty states that no more than 100 passengers (plus support crew) can go ashore at any landing site at any one time. Also, landings have to be prebooked, so if plans change the ship may have to travel further to find one that is available. (Ships with over 500 passengers aren't allowed to land at all.)

By contrast, a vessel taking up to 200 passengers may be called an expedition ship. Smaller ones set a limit of 100 or fewer for Antarctica, so that everybody can go ashore at once. Otherwise you must await your group's turn to land. Inevitably, your time ashore is more limited if you choose a larger ship. Mustering and disembarking by means of the Zodiacs (and everything else) takes longer.

The ship size also affects the outside/inside balance. Expedition ships are much more focused on the world outside and on making nimble landings in remoter spots, whereas cruise ships offer more facilities, provide more onboard entertainment and perhaps offer access to a gym or spa. Depending on your expectations of comfort, you might find an expedition ship somewhat spartan – or it may create exactly the atmosphere of exploration that you are seeking.

Above all, unlike modern planes and trains, each ship has its own individual sub-culture, atmosphere and style. Some encourage passengers to visit the bridge, others don't allow passengers on the foredeck. Some mix everybody together in large tables in a single dining-room, others offer more formal dining at separate tables in a choice of restaurants. If having a range of facilities and entertainment on board is important to you, that may make a larger ship attractive.

The age of the ship affects cabin comfort. Older vessels may have multi-berth cabins, some windowless, others with portholes, and only their priciest cabins boast any kind of balcony. By contrast, some modern ships have balconies almost throughout (for passengers, not for crew) and some have a few single cabins. Try to anticipate how much time you will spend in your cabin. If it's mainly for sleeping, then having a balcony may seem much less important: you will always get a better view from the observation lounge or deck – especially if the whales or icebergs are on the other side of the ship. But if you expect to spend much daytime in the cabin, then its creature comforts may matter to you more.

The ratio of staff to passengers is an important statistic, and tends to be high, perhaps in the range 1:2 or even 1:1. This is a major element in why Antarctic cruises are so expensive compared with voyages in less hostile waters. The three main categories are: the ship's crew that operate the vessel, 'hotel' staff that service the cabins and restaurants, and guides or naturalists. The latter give lectures, help with bird-spotting and whale-watching from the decks and go ashore with passengers in the Zodiacs. For many readers, easy access to the naturalists may be the most important factor.

Icebreaker at work in the Ross Sea

The language and culture of the ship varies widely. English is normally spoken everywhere, especially on the bridge and among the crew, but announcements will normally be made in the language of the ship first, and if need be afterwards in English. The naturalists will normally use a single language on each excursion, though most have some fluency in a second language. So any language mix among passengers will affect how the groups are arranged for Zodiac cruises and landings.

Other aspects of the ship's design may matter. For example larger ships tend to have deeper draughts. Requiring deeper water, they cannot reach landing sites accessible to nimbler ships, or may have to anchor far from the site for access by Zodiac. They also have larger engines, making for higher cruising speeds and reducing the time that you spend in the Drake Passage. If motion sickness is a major concern, it's worth finding out about the ship's stabilisers. However, for nights at sea, the position of your cabin may matter at least as much as your choice of ship: see page 90.

Depending on your itinerary, it *may* be important to know if your ship has ice-breaking capabilities. Three main features contribute to this:
• the shape of the hull, so that it can rise clear of the ice and bear down on it
• strengthening of the hull, especially at the front (bow)
• enough engine power to drive through sea ice.

Different countries and shipping companies use different notations for ice-breaking capability. For ships built since 2007, the international Polar Class system has gained support, with a simple range from 1 (most capable) to 7 (least capable). Even the lowest rated PC7 can cope with summer/autumn operation in thin first-year ice. As of 2023 no PC1s had yet been built, and only one PC2-rated ship was in service: Ponant's *Commandant Charcot* which has been taking cruise passengers to the North Pole since July 2022. It reached the southernmost navigable latitude of 78° 44' in the Ross Sea in February 2022.

However, vessels with lesser ratings still have good ice-breaking capability and can operate in extreme polar waters. For example the South African ship *Agulhas II* was the mother ship for the successful Endurance22 expedition. It is rated PC5 and coped with the Weddell Sea in February/March 2022: see page 82. And there is an annual requirement for serious ice-breaking to allow fuel and supply ships to reach the research stations for their Antarctic winter work. The US Operation Deep Freeze has to forge a navigable channel through many miles of ice up to 21 feet (6·5 m) thick to keep open a supply line to McMurdo Station, Antarctica's largest base in the Ross Sea.

Some ships carry helicopters on certain departures. In view of the weather and sea ice, ferrying passengers by helicopter may make all the difference to the chances of landing near a colony of Emperor penguins, for example on Snow Hill Island. To avoid disturbance to wildlife, passengers may need to hike a fair distance after landing, but obviously helicopters are noisy and create pollution which you may prefer to avoid.

A typical day onboard

Before firming up your booking, it's worth trying to picture how you'll be spending time on board. Don't underestimate how long you will be at sea: the map on page 25 shows a circuit of over 3000 miles/4830 km *excluding* local cruising at destination. At a typical cruising speed that represents nearly 200 hours (8 days and nights) at sea just to connect the three locations. Some of this happens while you're asleep, and clearly ships with larger engines cruise faster than others, but both excursions and landings are limited by sheer geography. All cruise ships offer activities during days at sea, e.g. lectures, entertainments and social activities depending on the size of the ship, its facilities and traditions.

Sea days typically will feature many briefings, most with attendance mandatory. In the early days these will include lifeboat drill, biosecurity, IAATO rules and how all this affects landings, including minimum distances to be kept from the wildlife. There will also be advice on how to board and disembark from the Zodiacs, equipment issue and briefing for any specialist activities, and so on.

As well as practical briefings, expect lectures on topics of general Antarctic interest, depending on the specialisms of the naturalists on board. Examples include the formation of glaciers, how to identify seabirds, the life cycles of penguins, seals and whales, research on climate change and the history of exploration. These lectures are optional, but make a fascinating complement to the trip, usually well illustrated by images and videos.

Excursions days are very different. Trips are made typically twice daily, usually from two different anchorages. Often at least one is a landing trip and the other may be a cruise in a Zodiac: see photos on pages 12 and 18. Zodiacs are small boats driven by outboard engines: their rigid body has inflatable tubes upon which up to ten passengers can sit. They can approach close to icebergs and to wildlife and are also used to make landings. Expect a detailed briefing in advance, often the day before, about the next day's activities and landing site. This will be mandatory, and ensures that you know what to expect and what to take with you.

MV Ortelius,
an ice-strengthened
expedition ship

ORTELIUS

Landing trips may include various lengths of walks, from short ones to reach a penguin colony to longer walks to reach viewpoints or even to replicate the last section of Shackleton's famous hike across South Georgia: see page 78. Where the hike is strenuous, there will typically be an option for a shorter, flatter walk or to stay near the landing site and observe the wildlife and scenery.

Only on the smallest of ships (under 100 passengers) can you all go ashore at once; otherwise groups take their turns. On all ships there may be a delay of up to an hour after anchoring while crew land to scout out the site, perhaps placing flags or markers to indicate where walking is permitted and to prevent visitors from disturbing animals. Sometimes they may need to prepare physically for safe access, for example by cutting steps in steep ice or snow.

Specialist activities

Depending on which operator and vessel you choose, specialist activities may be available, usually at extra cost. So if sea kayaking, camping on ice or cross-country skiing is a priority to you, identify that early on and consider it alongside dates, costs and itinerary. It may also affect what clothing and rucksacks you need to take.

Check whether previous experience of the activity is recommended or required. For example, if you want to scuba-dive in Antarctic waters you will need documented experience of dry-suit diving before you could be accepted. However, a complete novice may be allowed to go snow-shoeing. To permit you to perform a 'polar plunge' (brief total immersion in the ocean), some ships require a recent electrocardiogram – and so on. Check on the current biosecurity rules that may limit what is on offer.

Bear in mind that even if you have booked and paid in advance, none of these options will be guaranteed. The equipment and staff will be on board, but ultimately the captain decides which landings can be made, based on the weather and sea state on the day. Even then, the group leader has to decide whether it is safe for the group to proceed in the light of people's skills and experience and the prevailing conditions. Although payment should be refunded if a paid-for activity can't go ahead, it's better to be prepared for uncertainty than to set your heart on anything.

Depending on the operator, such activities may be included in the price, charged at modest rates or highly priced. For example, kayaking may be charged at a couple of hundred dollars per session. To experience several adventurous activities, seek an expedition ship that brands its cruise as 'base camp'. These typically offer a menu of activities such as kayaking, scuba diving, camping, mountaineering, skiing, snowboarding or snow-shoeing. Citizen science activities may let you contribute to data collection.

Humpback whale diving close to kayakers

Teams on the Shackleton Traverse approaching Trident Col

Others offer a 'Shackleton hike', but this is normally only from Fortuna Bay to Stromness – just the last 3·7 miles of the mountainous, glacier-strewn 22-mile hike described on page 78. Bundling the activities into the price may sound like an amazing bargain, but scrutinise the itinerary with care. If you spend many days at sea when these activities are impossible, or if the weather is unsuitable once you are on location, the opportunities may be very limited and the bargain illusory.

Medical condition and travel insurance

All operators will require information on your medical condition and fitness to travel and land. This may range from a simple self-declaration to an onerous medical form to be completed by your doctor. Medical facilities available on board vary from ship to ship, but obviously they are limited. Bearing in mind how remote you will be from any land-based hospital, it is essential to have excellent travel insurance, preferably with unlimited medical evacuation costs. If you already have annual worldwide travel cover, check whether it includes Antarctic cruising. Depending on your age and medical history, suitable insurance may be very expensive, but it is essential. Ensure that your cancellation insurance is generous enough to cover your cruise in full.

Biosecurity and the Antarctic environment

Biosecurity is a general term for measures taken to prevent the introduction of harmful organisms. In the Antarctic context *all* non-native species are adverse, because when introduced they disrupt the ecosystem, and some species are highly invasive. IAATO recommends rigorous decontamination practices to avoid accidental introduction of non-native seeds, insects or diseases. Precautions will be taken mainly on board ship (and for boots, before boarding a plane, see the photo on page 26). It's useful to be aware of the issues before you make purchasing decisions at home.

All your equipment and clothing must be clean before you pack it. If you are taking clothing that you have worn while hiking or visiting a farm you should be especially careful to check pockets and any velcro closures. Check and clean the tips of any walking poles or camera tripods and clean boots from the inside, removing insoles. Anything you have bought new to take to Antarctica won't need to be cleaned, reducing the time you need to spend on all this.

While on board, you will have at least one briefing session on biosecurity with access to vacuum cleaners and other equipment to decontaminate your clothing and equipment. Expect to have your efforts inspected and any omissions pointed out for you to remedy. Before and after landing trips, you can expect to walk through a footbath, and there may also be brush-scrubbers to help clean your rubber boots. Never take food ashore and be extremely careful not to drop anything.

South Georgia pintail duck

South Georgia makes an instructive example. From 1775 when Captain Cook visited (see page 23), sealing and whaling ships used to stop there and they accidentally introduced mice and rats. This devastated the native bird population which, free of predators, had always laid its eggs on the ground or in burrows. For the rodents, this was a huge, easy food source, and since the island had no species to prey upon rodents, their population exploded. Many bird species were decimated or facing extinction, and two endemic species, the South Georgia pipit and pintail duck, were confined to a few tiny offshore island which were rodent-free.

In 2011 the world's largest anti-invasive species project began the massive task of eliminating rodents by dropping poisoned bait from helicopters. The extreme weather and steep terrain made flying difficult, and glacial retreat was in danger of enlarging the rat-infested area. By 2018 the battle had been won, and repeated monitoring by specially trained dogs, who walked over 1000 miles (1610 km) with their handlers, allowed the announcement that the island was finally rodent-free. The restoration of habitat allowed the bird population to recover, including the endemic South Georgia pipits and pintails: see the photo above.

The project had cost about USD 13 million/ GBP 10 million. This demonstrates that prevention is much cheaper and more sustainable than elimination; we all share a responsibility to avoid harm to the places that we visit. It is understandable, then, that biosecurity is stricter for South Georgia than for Antarctica. Fresh decontamination is needed before each landing site, whereas for Antarctic landings it may suffice to do it once, thoroughly, although boot washes are always a mandatory part of disembarking and embarking. Since the rules often change in response to events, always be guided by IAATO and their agents.

2 Experience Antarctica

This section focuses on the sights, sounds and smells that you will experience on any Antarctic visit. For some, the main attraction is the astonishing wildlife and its adaptations, for others it's the otherworldly beauty of its scenery with icebergs of different shapes, sizes and colours. Others again want to understand the continent's role in the world's climate and ocean levels. Whatever your interests, gaining some knowledge and understanding before you go will help you to make the most of your visit.

A short book cannot be comprehensive: please consider our suggestions for further reading on pages 94-5. We strongly recommend Lowen's *Antarctic Wildlife* as a superlative field guide, helpfully organised by location (Beagle Channel, Drake Passage and Antarctic Peninsula). After our wildlife section below, we examine frozen water in its many forms, especially icebergs and pack ice. Part 2 ends with a short section on the global context and the impact of changes in Antarctica.

Wildlife

Below we introduce the main species of flying seabirds, and also of penguins. Which species of penguin, and whether you'll see adults, chicks or both depends on what stage of the breeding cycle they have reached. In turn, this depends on when and where you go: see Part 1. However, we begin with krill, because it's the key species on which the others all rely. After krill and birds, we move on to mammals – seals, dolphins and whales.

First we begin with the cornerstone species for the abundance of life in Antarctic waters. Krill is a tiny shrimp-like crustacean with 11 pairs of legs that you may never see without help. It is the primary food source for penguins, seals and whales – as well as for many other animals such as squid and fish. Anything that threatens the krill supply is a serious threat to all the larger animals that consume it. Threats includes not only rises in ocean temperature, but also human activity such as factory ships that harvest krill on an industrial scale. People use krill in aquaculture, as bait for sports fishing and to create krill oil and supplements (rich in Omega 3).

Antarctic krill (Euphausia superba)

Krill feed on plankton, and they can dive to depths of 2 km or more as part of their daily migration. They are photo-luminescent so they can see each other even in the darkness of the deeps. The upsurge of currents in Antarctica creates an abundance of plankton and krill which can reach densities of 60,000 animals per cubic metre.

Antarctic krill make up the world's largest biomass, currently about 379 million tonnes. The Southern Ocean is one of the world's largest carbon sinks, as well as largest fishing grounds, and krill are an important agent in this carbon capture. They move in vast swarms, and their carbon-rich faecal pellets sink en masse, taking the carbon to a deep, safe place. So they play an important role in the global environment and climate.

Krill at night, deep in the ocean

Seabirds

Here are five seabird groups that you may see in the Drake Passage and around the Antarctic Peninsula. Both the Falklands and South Georgia have many additional species not covered here. Although the Beagle Channel is ideal for starting to recognise bird species, some ships' departure arrangements make it difficult or impossible to be on deck while it is still light, so below we focus more on the Drake and Peninsula.

Antarctic tern

While on board, and especially during the long crossing of the Drake, the two best places for bird-watching are the bridge (or as close to it as you are allowed) and also the stern of the boat where birds sometimes forage or float around in the lee of the ship. If you've invested in good binoculars, you will experience the massive benefit; if you haven't, you may come to regret it. Most ships will have specialists in bird identification: seek their help.

We start with more familiar seabird groups and work outwards. Most readers will know seagulls from home, and perhaps will have read about albatrosses. Some other groups – petrels and sheathbills – may be unfamiliar. Discerning and experienced bird-watchers should probably skip this section, and consult instead a proper field guide such as Lowen's book.

| Wandering albatross 330 cm/10 ft 10 in | Black-browed albatross 235 cm/7 ft 9 in | Southern giant petrel 190 cm/6 ft 3 in | Kelp gull 135 cm/4 ft 5 in | Cape petrel 85 cm/2 ft 10 in | Wilson's storm petrel 40 cm/1 ft 4 in |

Typical wingspans, ranging from Wandering albatross to Wilson's storm petrel

Relative novices should start by learning to identify a few of the commoner species. The size of a bird is a very useful clue. For this reason, we quote wingspans and body lengths, but in centimetres only in the main text to avoid a mass of awkward conversions. The graphic above gives you a quick idea of the range of sizes in both imperial and metric units.

Gulls, skuas and terns

The Kelp gull is the commonest and largest gull in the region, and the only one that breeds on the Peninsula. It feeds mainly on limpets, although it also preys upon penguin and tern nests. It is a large bird, 55-65 cm in length, wingspan as above. They make a handy size comparison for other birds.

In their breeding plumage, adults have smart black wings with narrow white edges and white heads and tails, with a red spot under the bill. Immature birds are much less striking and Kelp gulls can take two to three years to achieve their adult plumage. Until then, they are dingier and brownish, and could be confused with skuas.

Kelp gull

Skuas are large, thick-necked gull-like birds, generally brownish with white flashes on their wings. Four species exist (Chilean, Southern, Brown and South polar), but the differences in size and shape are subtle; identifying them takes practice and knowledge of colour variants (pale, intermediate and dark). Skuas are the pirates of the avian world, living off other birds rather than catching their own food. Brown skuas are as large as Kelp gulls, and steal their food by harrassing them until they release their catch. Brown skuas also hang around penguin colonies, stealing unguarded eggs.

Brown skua

Terns are pale, slender, graceful birds and you may see two kinds, Arctic (below) and Antarctic (page 34). Both have a black cap, red bill and long forked tail. The slightly smaller Arctic tern has shorter legs and a slender bill, but with a slightly larger wingspan, and you're more likely to see it out at sea. Antarctic terns are common around Peninsula landing sites.

Arctic terns have an amazing life cycle: they breed in the Arctic summer, then fly to the Antarctic summer – only to return before its winter sets in. This makes an annual round trip of some 24,000 miles/38,000 km. They are long-lived, about 20 years or so, during which they cover nearly half a million miles (800,000 km).

Arctic tern

Albatrosses and fulmars

The first albatross you will see is the Black-browed: it's a large bird, 80-95 cm long with a wingspan of 220-250 cm, and may visit your ship from the Beagle Channel onwards. It is both larger than a Kelp gull and has a much greater wingspan (by a metre), a black tail and stiff-winged flight. Albatross wings look very thin in proportion to their bodies, and the Black-browed has wings that are dark above with white bands on the underside. Albatrosses seem to glide effortlessly, especially in strong winds.

You may see many other kinds of albatross both at sea and around the sub-Antarctic islands. In the Drake Passage look out for the impressive Wandering albatross, whose wingspan (305 to 355 cm) is the greatest of any living bird: see page 37. The name is apt: tracking studies have reported one bird that flew 15,500 miles/25,000 km in nine weeks. When in flight, it achieved an average speed of 34 mph/55 kph.

Albatross wingspan

The Wandering albatross has an outstanding wingspan that makes identification easy. The only possible confusion is with a Royal albatross which has two variants, Southern and (rare) Northern Royals. Their bodies are shorter and their wingspans very slightly smaller (300-350 cm). If in doubt, ask an onboard naturalist.

Albatrosses provide great sightings for visiting cruise ships, but they are in serious danger from fishing vessels which use longlines. At one time longline hooks were drowning at least 100,000 albatrosses every year, and without a great conservation effort, these magnificent birds may face extinction: see page 95 for how to help.

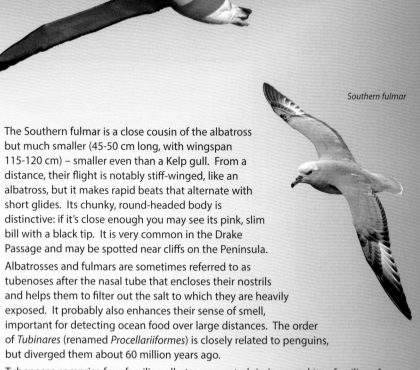

Wandering albatross

Southern fulmar

The Southern fulmar is a close cousin of the albatross but much smaller (45-50 cm long, with wingspan 115-120 cm) – smaller even than a Kelp gull. From a distance, their flight is notably stiff-winged, like an albatross, but it makes rapid beats that alternate with short glides. Its chunky, round-headed body is distinctive: if it's close enough you may see its pink, slim bill with a black tip. It is very common in the Drake Passage and may be spotted near cliffs on the Peninsula.

Albatrosses and fulmars are sometimes referred to as tubenoses after the nasal tube that encloses their nostrils and helps them to filter out the salt to which they are heavily exposed. It probably also enhances their sense of smell, important for detecting ocean food over large distances. The order of *Tubinares* (renamed *Procellariiformes*) is closely related to penguins, but diverged them about 60 million years ago.

Tubenoses comprise four families: albatrosses, petrels/prions, and two families of storm petrel (northern and southern hemisphere). They all tend to be long-lived and monogamous, with long-term pair bonds. Usually they lay and hatch a single egg each year, although large albatrosses may lay only once every two years.

Petrels and prions

In the Drake and around the Peninsula, look out for Cape petrels, which are common and sometimes accompany ships, which means you might get a close view. Although its flight pattern is like that of the Southern fulmar, it is smaller, length about 35-40 cm and wingspan 80-90 cm. It has much shorter wings and its wings sport distinctively patterned plumage. Mottled white wingtop patterns contrast with a very dark brown head; its underparts are mostly white fringed with dark brown. Its smart plumage gives rise to its Spanish name – Pintado (painted) petrel.

Cape petrel

South of the Antarctic Convergence (see page 6) you may start to see the somewhat similar Antarctic petrel and, as you approach the Peninsula, perhaps your first Snow petrel, the elegant 'angel of Antarctica'. This otherwise snow-white bird has black eyes and a short beak. Although similar in size to a Cape petrel it appears slimmer, with narrower wings.

Snow petrel

Storm petrels are generally brown with white relief. Try to spot the tiny Wilson's storm petrel – its body is half the length of a Cape, and its wingspan only 40 cm. In flight its wings look rounded and its legs dangle. You may even see it seeming to patter lightly across the sea, as if walking on water. The name petrel means 'little Peter', after the apostle Peter. Most petrels remain at sea almost year-round, landing only to dig burrows in which they lay their eggs, for protection from skuas.

The largest of all petrels are the giant petrels (Northern and Southern), which have a stocky body, length 85-95 cm and wingspan 170-210 cm. Unlike albatrosses and smaller petrels, they forage both on land and sea, able to kill birds as large as King penguins and scavenging whatever they find in seal colonies. Southern giant petrels breed as far south as the Peninsula. Northerns are less common than Southerns, and more likely to be seen in the Drake Passage.

Prions are are small blue-grey petrels (also known as whalebirds) with plumage whose colouring often matches the sea. As a result, these fast-flying birds can seem to disappear and reappear against the blue-grey waves. They are gregarious, so expect to see mixed flocks of both Antarctic and Slender-billed prions with perhaps a few Blue petrels in the mix.

Southern giant petrel

Shags and sheathbills

Around the Antarctic coast you may see smart white-fronted birds called Antarctic shag. Generally they look a bit like winged penguins, and they can fly as well as swim. They are about 75 cm long, with a long, slender neck and blue eye-ring, with a yellow patch of rough facial skin. Juveniles are browner and much less colourful. Very similar birds known as Imperial shag may be seen in the Beagle Channel.

The Snowy sheathbill is a plump, white bird that hangs around penguin colonies, harrassing parent penguins, scavenging for food scraps and stealing unguarded eggs. Slightly larger than a pigeon, it has a much heavier bill encased in a bony sheath. Although they breed solely in Antarctica, their feet are not webbed so they like to stay dry.

Nesting Antarctic shag being tormented by a Gentoo penguin

Emperor 120 cm	King 90 cm	Gentoo 80 -85 cm	Chinstrap 70-75 cm	Adélie 70 cm	Magellanic 65-70 cm	Macaroni 70 cm	Rockhopper 50 cm

100 cm
39 in

50 cm
20 in

Penguins

Penguins are widely distributed over the southern hemisphere ranging from the equator (Ecuador) to South Africa and the Antarctic. The fossil record suggests that about 40 species have ever lived, including giant penguins that are long extinct. Nowadays 17-19 penguin species are recognised, the precise number depending on the outcome of debate about how many rockhopper species there are.

Penguins are the most sociable of all birds, living in colonies that are known as rookeries or huddles, or – when swimming – a raft. When walking, they may be called a waddle, march, muster or parade. Large colonies may have thousands, or even millions, of birds. They nest, travel and feed together, which helps them to resist their many predators. In past centuries, predators included humans (see page 63), but nowadays their main predators are skuas, giant petrels, Leopard seals and Orcas.

Although technically flightless, penguins have remarkable adaptations to life in the water: their superb streamlining lets them 'fly through the water' and fused bones turn their 'wings' into efficient paddles. They contract their feathers after entering the water to expel trapped air: this not only helps swimming by reducing their buoyancy, it also creates clouds of bubbles – a useful screen from predator pursuit.

A huddle of Kings

A penguin waterproofs its feathers using oil from the uropygial gland near its tail. You may see them using their bills to stimulate the oil flow, and spread it on their feathers. It gives them extremely effective protection against the icy water. However, when they are moulting they have to replace all their feathers, which is extremely energy-sapping. It's important to avoid stressing them during this process.

A King preening

Penguins range in size from under 50 cm to over 130 cm, and are described below in ascending height order. Their colonies are widespread in the Antarctic Peninsula, with ice-intolerant species such as Gentoo and Chinstrap in the north and west, whereas the ice-dependent Adélies tend towards the colder south and east. Emperors occur only in remote colonies, of which Snow Hill Island is the least inaccessible. King penguins are found in great numbers on South Georgia, with vagrants possible elsewhere.

The Southern rockhopper is the smallest, but you are unlikely to see it unless the odd straggler appears in the Beagle Channel or Drake Passage, or unless you visit the Falklands. Its yellow/black punk hair is distinctive, as is its blunt red bill: see below.

Magellanic penguins

Don't confuse it with the taller, stockier Macaroni, which has golden streamers that droop from its forehead and a bulbous red bill. Both are comparatively rare, but you might spot a few Macaronis among a colony of Chinstraps or other penguins on the South Shetlands. The Magellanic (65-70 cm) is more likely to be seen in the Beagle Channel than further south, and has a distinctive large white stripe framing its cheek, as well as white on its underbody and back.

Rockhopper penguin, Falklands

Adélie penguins are also about 70 cm tall but adults have white rings encircling their eyes and an otherwise black, almost triangular head. They are gregarious and squabblesome, and delightful to watch with their extreme waddle. They appear cautious before entering the water and may rocket out of the sea with an athletic leap. They have the fastest of all penguin breeding cycles and build nests from stones, frequently stealing and squabbling over stones from other nests.

Adélie rocketing out of the sea

The Chinstrap is named after its thin black facial stripe. Its feet are pink above and black below, which may help with camouflage while swimming. Chinstraps are slightly taller than Adélies, and common around the Peninsula. They are surprisingly keen hikers, and may create colonies high on mountain slopes. They use their strong bills like an ice-axe, to help them climb the icy terrain.

Third largest of the penguin species is the Gentoo, common on the South Shetlands and the western Antarctic Peninsula. They have a distinctive white flash above the eyes and an otherwise black head with red bill: see the photo on page 17. Like Adélies, Gentoos build nests from stones, preferring to pilfer pebbles from other nests than to find their own. They have various techniques to distract and deceive.

Chinstrap penguin

The King penguin is a majestic tall bird, with orange-gold neck and ear patches. Their colouring varies, being strongest in adults in the breeding season, and paler at other times and in juveniles. South Georgia is the place to see colonies with hundreds of thousands: the sight, sound and smell is unforgettable.

The King penguin breeding cycle is unusual: they take two months to incubate eggs and 50 weeks to raise chicks, so they breed only twice in three years. From April to September the chicks are made to fast, then the parents feed them up and desert them once fledged. Kings don't breed in Antarctica and are seldom seen there.

The eye of the King

The penguin's pupil looks squareish and small in daylight: see the foot of page 41. When diving deeply, it expands hugely. Kings routinely dive to depths of over 100 m (330 ft), and on occasion they go three times that deep. Emperors (see below) have recorded depths of 500 m. The light level in the abyss is less than that of starlight, so they enhance their vision by enlarging the pupil to cover the entire area of the eye.

The Emperor is the largest of all penguins, but you are unlikely to see any unless your itinerary is aimed at a breeding colony such as Snow Hill Island in the Weddell Sea. Adults weigh 23 to 45 kg and their head colouring resembles a paler version of the King's. Their bodies are much larger and their heads look small in proportion. This is the only bird that breeds in the Antarctic winter, and the parents' close co-operation is legendary: see the panel.

For safety from predators, the breeding colony is set up afresh each year on newly formed sea ice. To reach it, they make a long journey (up to 60 miles/100 km), either waddling or 'tobogganing'– sliding on their bellies, propelled by strongly clawed toes and bill. In April each year they pair up: to cement their courtship, they make synchronised, movements and trumpet and coo in duet.

Once breeding is complete, the Emperors all return to the sea to feed from January to March, before repeating the process the next year. Their story was filmed over 11 months by a team from the BBC. For details of McCrae's book and of the documentary, see page 95.

Parental devotion through Antarctic winter

After mating, in May the female lays her single egg, an energy-sapping process. Having lost up to 25% of her body weight, she must return to the open sea to feed. Meanwhile the father incubates the egg in the brood pouch above his feet for 9-10 weeks. Throughout June and July he endures the brutal blizzards of darkest mid-winter on an empty stomach. He survives winds of 125 mph/200 kph and temperatures down to -50 °C by forming a massive huddle with other fathers, rotating positions to distribute the heat fairly.

When the chicks start to hatch in August, their survival depends on the mothers returning from the sea, fat and healthy, ready to regurgitate lots of fish. Once reunited, the father gently passes the precious egg (or newly hatched chick) to the mother's brood pouch. Finally, after four months of fasting, he can leave to feed.

The chicks grow at an incredible pace and by October they are left behind while both parents go fishing to feed them, so they form mini huddles for warmth and comfort. Once spring starts to warm up, both adults and their downy chicks start to moult. It's only once moulting is complete that the chicks are viable. By December, the pack ice is breaking up and they return to the sea.

Left: Emperor juvenile squawking for its parents
Above: Emperor chick with both parents

Seals

Of the six species of seals that inhabit Antarctica, five are true blubber seals – namely the Southern elephant, Weddell, Crabeater, Ross and Leopard, and the sixth is the Fur seal. Most seal females tend to be a bit larger than the males, but the reverse is true of Elephant and Fur seals. Seals often look ungainly on land, but they are elegant swimmers and divers, superb at hunting fish, krill and squid. They are also skilful at evading predators, of which the greatest threat is the Orca.

The Southern elephant is the world's largest seal, with males up to 5·8 metres (19 ft) long and weighing up to 3·7 tonnes. Females are much smaller, at 350-900 kg. Of the estimated 400,000 individuals, about half breed on South Georgia. The young male in the photo above is relaxing on the beach. They spend most of their time at sea and are superb swimmers and divers, outperforming most whales. They typically reach depths of 400 -1000 m, but have been recorded at an amazing 2·4 km.

Their name comes from the bull's proboscis which looks more like a trunk after it grows with age. The bull inflates it to resonate and amplify his bellowing at a rival. The alpha male defends his territory fiercely with threat postures, vocalising and lunging at challengers. The strongest bull gathers a harem of up to 100 females and drives out weaker males. The latter may try to mate if the beachmaster's attention is distracted, but they are often unsuccessful. Only about 1% of males get to mate during their entire lives, so the females are impregnated only by the strongest, most dominant males. Natural selection is fierce and the beachmasters seldom maintain their position for more than one season.

In October, pregnant females return to the beaches where they were born, and give birth soon afterwards. They nurse the pups for three weeks or so, but before weaning is complete, they mate and return to the sea in November to restore lost body weight. However delayed implantation means that the next pup won't come to term until the following year, allowing a 7-9 month gestation period to synchronise with an annual breeding cycle.

Two Elephant seal bulls vying for dominance

Weddell seal pup on sea ice

Weddell seals are named after James Weddell (see page 62) and they are the world's southernmost breeding seal, ranging as far as 78° S in the Ross Sea. The females measure about 3·3 m and weigh 450 kg or so, males slightly less. They are elite divers, somehow lowering their metabolic rate so they can routinely spend 15-20 minutes per dive and on occasion managing 60-80 minutes. This lets them make deep foraging dives, typically 100-350 m deep, but a depth of 741 m has been recorded.

These long dives beneath the ice are to find food, but their incredible duration also allows time to locate and use air holes on return to the surface. If need be, their sharp teeth can gnaw holes in the ice. Weddell seals often give birth on the ice in September/October. They feed mainly on Antarctic cod, but also take krill and squid.

Leopard seals are a little smaller, adult males averaging about 2·8 m and 325 kg with females a little larger and heavier. Their heads have an almost reptilian shape with a sinister 'smiling' upturn at the corners of the mouth, and savage-looking teeth. Named after their pattern of spots, they are (like actual leopards) solitary predators. You may see them lying on an ice floe.

In addition to eating fish, squid and krill, Leopard seals prey upon penguins and will also take Crabeater seals, especially juveniles. They are considered dangerous to humans, having attacked people walking on sea ice and having drowned at least one diver. The exact population is unknown: one estimate suggests a range of 220,000 to 440,000.

Crabeaters don't eat crabs, but mainly krill, squid and fish. They outnumber all the other seal species combined with about 4 to 8 million individuals. They are slim and fast-moving, spending their whole lives on and below the pack ice. Males are typically 2·6 metres long and weigh about 225 kg, females a little larger. Their main predator is

Leopard seal, a solitary predator

the Leopard seal, and Crabeaters often haul out on ice floes to escape them. Like most seals, their pups are born in the spring.

The Ross seal is slightly smaller than the Crabeater – up to 2·4 m long and 200 kg. They are hard to study, the population of about 40,000 being widely dispersed. They spend most of their time on the pack ice, but also forage in the Southern Ocean, returning for pupping and breeding in November and December. They are named after James Clark Ross who was the first to collect a specimen in 1841.

Finally, the Antarctic fur seal resembles a sea lion, rather than a true seal, and is easily recognised by its visible outer ears, cute face, and ability to 'stand' on its rear flippers. Adult males are about 1·8 m long with average weight 188 kg, with females much smaller at about 1·3 m, and one fifth the weight of a male. Their rear flippers can face both ways (see photo below), and at 12 mph/ 20 kph they can easily outrun a human on rough terrain. Since their teeth are sharp and their bite full of bacteria, they should be treated with respect and given plenty of space.

Fur seals have visible ears (above) and opposable rear flippers (below)

Whales and dolphins

Cetaceans (whales and dolphins) are of two kinds: baleen whales, which filter small crustaceans such as krill using baleen (the comb-like structures that line their jaws), and toothed whales (including dolphins) which have jaws with teeth. Baleens include the Blue whale, the largest animal that has ever lived, which can weigh up to 180-200 tonnes and are up to 33 m/100 ft long. Fin whales weigh up to 120 tonnes and are 25-27 metres long, and they also rely on baleen.

Head of a Southern right whale, showing its baleen

The smaller Humpbacks (typically 14-17 m), Southern right whales (11-16 m) and Minkes (smaller again at 8-10 m long) are all baleen whales. The 'right whale' was so-called because it swims slowly and was easily hunted. They may be spotted around the South Shetlands, their huge dark heads covered in calluses and their smooth bodies having no dorsal fin. Baleen is made of keratin, the same protein that is in your fingernails and hair. The comb-like structure filters huge quantities of seawater, retaining the krill and small fry: see the photo above.

Sadly, human greed meant that Blue whales were the first to be hunted nearly to extinction, and Fin whales are an endangered species. Over 750,000 Fin whales were slaughtered in the southern hemisphere in the 20th century and, as for Blue whales, recovery is likely to be slow because their breeding cycle is so long.

Whales have tailfins (known as flukes) that move mainly vertically and provide powerful forward propulsion, though very subtle movements also help them to steer. Most whales have a dorsal fin (on their backs) for stability and two pectoral fins (on their undersides) that do most of the steering. However the position and size of these fins varies widely from one species to another. Unless you are lucky enough to see a whale breaching (leaping out of the water, see below) you will see only a tiny part of the swimming animal's back, so it's useful to know which fins to look for.

Humpback whale breaching

Of all the whale species in Antarctica, the one you are most likely to see is the Humpback – also one of the most widespread worldwide. Biologists know most about them partly because they are relatively easy to study – albeit tracking individuals moving over vast expanses of ocean is always difficult. They appear in Antarctica from mid-December onwards and are black above with white undersides to the flukes and fins. The photo on page 30 shows kayakers close to a Humpback diving, an experience that I was lucky enough to share and will never forget.

The main method of study used to be identification by photo, each animal being recognisable by its fluke (Humpback), head calluses (Southern right whales) or pointed snouts (Minke). Modern methods include many other techniques, including tags, drones, satellites and citizen science. Drones can carry petri dishes to collect samples from whale blows, helping scientists to know whether populations are mixing and helping them to deduce the main paths of migrations.

Whale migration is a bit of a mystery: see the panel. Whales found in the Antarctic ocean go south in summer to their prime feeding grounds, but in winter they migrate huge distances to breed in more tropical waters. Different groups go to different places: for example Humpbacks from the sub-Antarctic islands go up the Atlantic coast to Brazil, whereas those from the Antarctic Peninsula head up the Pacific coast all the way to Colombia and even Costa Rica, a round trip of over 11,000 miles (18,000 km). During these strenuous journeys, the animals are fasting. Each mother and calf migrates repeatedly until the calf is mature enough to travel alone.

Why do whales migrate?

The reason for these epic, energy-sapping journeys is unclear. At least four theories have been advanced and the truth may lie in some combination. There are counter-instances that challenge each theory:

- water is a less challenging environment for the calves to be born into
- going further north reduces the chances of attack by Orcas
- cold water saps the energy levels of the adults, as well as young
- maintaining their skin condition requires the blood to reach its surface, which it never does in cold water.

Toothed whales include Orcas and several other dolphins. The Orca (aka killer whale) is the world's largest dolphin and Antarctica's top predator. Their sleek muscular bodies range widely in size, with males from 4·5 to 9 metres in length and females a bit smaller. They may appear to be almost entirely black when swimming, when they reach speeds of up to 32 mph/50 kph. You may see whiteish patches on their heads and sides or glimpse their pale undersides.

Recent research suggests there may be three sub-species of Orca. Type A hunt in ice-free waters and feed mainly on Minke whales, whereas Type B are smaller, with a larger oval eye-patch and they feed mainly on seals. Type C are different again, and feed mainly on fish. Males have a prominent, acutely triangular dorsal fin, whereas those of females and juveniles are smaller, and more curved.

Orca family from L to R: a female, juvenile and male

Head of an Orca, Antarctica's top predator

Orcas display great intelligence and cooperation. They use bubble-netting – blowing lots of bubbles while circling a shoal of fish – to create a visual barrier that corrals the fish. Swimming in an upward spiral, the Orcas drive the fish up to the surface and can then feast on them. Although this is usually a collaboration, a single Orca has been filmed performing this on its own.

Orcas also prey upon penguins and seals, usually hunting as a pack. A lone seal on an ice floe is a favourite target. The Orcas often start by 'spy-hopping' (standing almost vertical in the sea for a good view of terrain and possible prey). Then they coordinate their swimming to create progressively larger waves that soon swamp the ice floe. Once the hapless seal is in the water, they devour it.

Of the other dolphin species, in the Drake you may sight Hourglass dolphins (length 1·4 to 1·9 m), in small pods perhaps bow-riding with your ship if you're lucky. The name refers to their narrow-waisted white ventral patch, and they have notably curvy, hooked back dorsal fins. In the Beagle Channel, you might see the tiny Commerson's dolphin with its rounded dorsal fin. At 1·2 to 1·7 m it is the smallest cetacean, and commoner than both Dusky and Peale's dolphins.

Hourglass dolphin

Frozen water

Antarctica has a wide range of frozen water: ice may be formed in fresh water or saline (salty). If mixed with lots of air, snow may be light and fluffy or, if heavily compressed, may form airless blue ice: see below.

How does snow turn into glacier ice on Antarctica? Freshly fallen snow consists of more air than snowflakes, with a density only 30-50% that of water. If the climate is cold enough, the fallen snow lies unmelted, and further snowfall builds up, month on month, year on year. Beneath about 1 m of snow, the consistency becomes more like granular sugar, to a depth of about 5 m, with density up to 60% that of water. Beneath that lies a layer of compacted, recrystallised snow which is denser again, up to 80% and known as *firn* or *névé*. Firn looks like wet sugar but is extremely hard to dig and shovel. Beneath it at depths of 300-350 m (985-1150 ft) lies the hard blue glacier ice, its upper parts containing trapped air bubbles.

From top to bottom, the column of frozen water varies in density from 30% to 90%. This is because the weight of the layers above exerts downward pressure, progressively squeezing out the trapped air. Because air scatters the light randomly, the upper layers tend to look white, whereas the base layers consists of solid blue glacier ice. Note that the diagram is schematic, and not to scale vertically.

0 m *not to scale*

Newly fallen snow

1 m
Granular, sugary snow

5 m
Firn/névé

70 m
Glacier ice with air bubbles

300–350 m
Clear, hard, blue glacier ice

Icebergs and ice shelves

Icebergs begin their lives as falling snow. Once enough snow has fallen on land, it is compressed by its own weight to form glaciers or ice sheets. Laid down over hundreds and thousands of years, these become massively compacted. Where a glacier forms on sloping ground, it becomes a huge frozen river that flows down towards the sea, descending inexorably under its own immense weight.

Glacier flow is very slow compared with running water in a river – typically only 1 m per day – but picks up speed when a layer of water forms beneath the glacier, lubricating and accelerating its passage over the rocky ground, eventually ending in the sea. Geothermal heat and movement friction cause melting at the base of a glacier, and surface water may percolate down to join the meltwater, accelerating its motion.

What happens when the ice meets the sea depends on the angle at which it is flowing. If it's nearly horizontal, it may float on the surface to form an ice shelf. However, if it's descending steeply, huge pieces will break off as icebergs – a process referred to as calving. In summer months you may be lucky enough to see this dramatic process from a Zodiac, from a safe distance. The sea is cold enough that the bergs can take a very long time to melt, often after travelling large distances and drifting into warmer water.

Triangular column on the point of calving

height <1 m	1-5 m	5-15 m	15-45 m	45-75 m
Growler	Bergy bit	Small	Medium	Large

Icebergs are given different names according to their diameters: the smallest ones – up to 1 m tall, up to 5 m in diameter – are called growlers and are dangerous to shipping because they are very difficult to spot in a swell and so much of their depth is concealed. Larger lumps (height up to 1·5 m) are called bergy bits and can be up to 15 m in diameter, with deep keels of unknown shape. Small icebergs are 5 to 15 m in height, and less of a danger because they show up on ship's radar systems.

The infamous *Titanic* disaster of 1912 was caused by its high-speed collision with a medium iceberg floating about 15-30 m (50-100 ft) above the waterline: contemporary estimates differed. The berg's weight has been calculated at about two million tons, and its submerged keel critically buckled the ship's hull. *Titanic* was steaming at 22 knots (41 kph) in a known risk area. On the dark night of 14 April, amid patches of fog and without binoculars, the crew spotted the berg too late to avoid it. Modern ships have radar and other safety systems that mean such bergs seldom pose danger nowadays.

Very large bergs (over 75 m/250 ft tall) are given a letter and number by the US National Ice Center, which tracks them by satellite. The letter identifies which Antarctic sector it falls in, and the number is a serial number within that sector. For example, A68 was the 68th berg to calve in the north-west sector (coded A): sectors B, C and D follow clockwise around the pole.

Sculptured shapes and colours inside an iceberg in Marguerite Bay

Antarctic ice sheets can push bergs out to sea to float for many miles. The action of warmth, weather and waves then shapes them. After cracks open up, they deepen and may split. The largest of all icebergs are the flat-topped tabular bergs. When huge pieces known as ice islands break off, they may be long-lived, persisting for up to 5 or 10 years. A gigantic ice sheet called Larsen B was stable for 10,000 years before it broke up over a few weeks in early 2002.

Ice shelves

Where a glacier flows off the land and manages to float without either melting or breaking off into bergs, it forms an ice shelf. Unlike the Arctic, Antarctica has many of these and their scale is enormous: the largest, the Ross Ice Shelf, is larger than the whole of Spain, and the thickest, the Ronne-Filchner, is more than 3 km (1·9 miles) thick. The ice shelves hold back the glaciers on their landward sides, delaying the glacial flow in a 'buttressing effect'. Ice shelves are vital to stabilising the Antarctic ice mass, but their contact with a warming ocean makes them vulnerable.

The map above shows the location of some of the most important ice shelves. The only area where bays remain free of ice is the north-west Peninsula, and this seems to reflect its relatively high air temperature, especially in summer. If significant surface melting happens in summer months, the shelf cannot survive, and scientists speak of the 'climatic limit of viability' of ice shelves. This roughly corresponds with an average annual temperature of about -9 °C (16 °F). In recent decades, this climatic limit has inexorably moved south.

In 2002, the collapse of Larsen B made the headlines, although it had long been predicted by the British Antarctic Survey. However, it happened sooner than expected, and satellite images showed the sudden loss of over 3200 sq km/ 1235 sq mi of ice over a period of 40 days.

In 2017 part of the larger Larsen C Ice Shelf broke off, creating A68 – one of the largest bergs recorded to date. Its massive size (5800 sq km/2240 sq mi) posed a major threat. It was drifting towards South Georgia, and (at over 100 km long by 20 km) was roughly the same size as the entire sub-Antarctic island. Had it collided, the effect on South Georgia's wildlife could have been catastrophic. Happily the currents took it some distance to the east, and it broke into smaller pieces before serious damage was done.

Water expands when it freezes, making ice less dense than water: see the panel opposite on density. But iceberg density varies more than you might expect. Everybody knows that what you see is only the 'tip of the iceberg', but the hidden proportion varies greatly. The thicker the ice shelf, the deeper and denser the 'keel' of any bergs that calve from it. The keels of large bergs can reach up to 500 m in depth, although 200-300 m is more usual – even on the massive ones.

Icebergs and density

The amount of air captive inside a berg is important in several ways: the more air, the more buoyant the berg and the higher its proportion visible above sea level. But the air is also responsible for a more obvious feature – their white colour. Inside bergs with plenty of air bubbles, white light is scattered and most of it reflected back to the human eye, making the iceberg appear white. Glacial debris can also contribute to this scattering. In very pure icebergs, with little or no trapped air or debris, the ice absorbs light from the red end of the spectrum and the blue remains, sometimes even turquoise. This effect is more pronounced on a cloudy day because there is less reflected sunlight.

Shape is affected by many factors: large calving events tend to create flat-topped or tabular bergs. Over the life of a berg, its shape can change dramatically. Recently calved bergs may have sharp corners and towers, but as they partly melt, or are sculpted by wind and waves, the shapes become smoother and more interesting. Older icebergs may have arches, contain internal lagoons or show fluting.

Because ice melts faster in water than in air, a berg may become top-heavy and overturn completely, depending on its shape and keel depth. Typically a berg that has turned turtle will have a rounded shape, often with some colourful algae and debris embedded.

Icebergs and density

Pure water has a density of exactly 1 gram/cubic centimetre (1 g/cc). Sea water is slightly denser because the salt adds to its weight without increasing its volume, but only by about 3% (1·03 g/cc). However, pure frozen water is 8% less dense than pure liquid water (about 0·92 g/cc) which is why ice cubes float in your glass of water. Icebergs are famous for hiding most of their bulk beneath the sea. This proportion varies widely, and can be anywhere in the range 50% - 99%, though 80-90% is more typical. The density of a berg depends not only on how compressed the ice became during its long journey to the sea, but also, crucially, on how much air has become trapped inside it.

Brash ice, ice floes and pack ice

Whilst water frozen into ice shelves and icebergs is fresh, salt water also freezes when the temperature falls far enough. Once the sea temperature drops below -1·8 C (29 °F) a film of grease-ice forms over the sea surface. Jagged floating fragments are known as brash ice and wind and waves may merge the fragments. As larger pieces of ice form, they are known as ice floes – flat, floating bits of ice at least a metre in diameter which are important for seals, penguins and others as places to rest, breed and hunt.

Wind and waves may merge the floes into larger areas known as pack ice. Persistent winds and currents can compress the pack into huge ice fields. Generally, the pack and the ice fields are always on the move unless they are landfast – i.e. securely attached to land; some sources call this fast-ice. Emperor penguins often set up their colonies on landfast ice, but if a big swell breaks the ice away, it can take the hapless colony with it.

In the past, explorers and scientists made long dog-sledging journeys over pack ice to reach Antarctic islands and coastline, and stranded seafarers sometimes crossed the pack ice to reach land. However, pack ice is subject to massive cumulative pressure from wind, waves and current. Dangerous gaps can open up unpredictably, as many explorers found to their cost. Human lives, dogs and vital supplies were often lost when water channels opened up suddenly in otherwise solid-looking expanses of pack ice. The pack ice plays a major role in the stories of the Heroic Age of Exploration: see Part 3.

Emperor penguins stranded on an ice floe

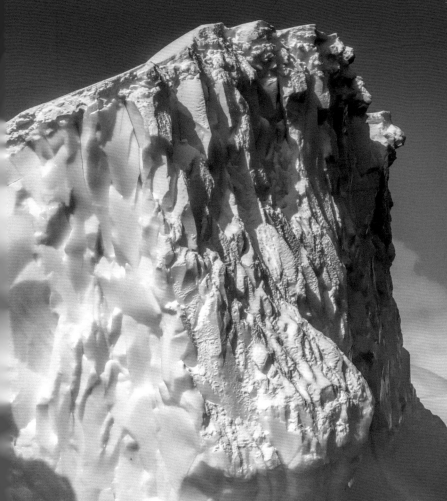

Zodiac seen through the arch in a large berg

Icebreaker moving through pack ice

Traditional ships were vulnerable to being trapped in the pack, especially before modern meteorology allowed better prediction of the danger areas. Being captured by the ice meant that they lost any ability to control their position, often drifting hundreds of miles, helplessly awaiting a spring thaw. In the Weddell Sea there's a powerful gyre – a clockwise current that carried many ships trapped near the Peninsula north-west. This current still takes large icebergs on a similar journey.

But drifting was only the start of a ship's mortal danger: an ice-nipped ship was subject to immense and changing pressures that could crush the strongest timbers. After *Endurance* was trapped in January 1915, her long north-westerly drift was accompanied by mounting structural damage that ended only in November when she finally sank: see page 74.

Modern ice-breakers avoid the V-shaped hull of traditional shipbuilding. Instead they have a rounded, thickened shape so that the bow rises above the sea ice. They can then use the ship's weight and powerful engine thrust to bear down on it and smash open a channel.

We've already seen that the winter formation of sea ice can double the size of the continent, but the extent of this ice varies widely from year to year – another factor that may force Antarctic cruises to vary their itineraries. Cruise ships need to be able to cope with first-year pack ice. However, where pack ice has formed in a particularly cold or sheltered bay, it may not melt throughout the summer and then it becomes cumulatively thicker, year on year. It takes an ice-strengthened ships or even an ice-breaker to cope with multi-year ice.

However, Antarctic sea ice is generally seasonal: it waxes and wanes on an annual cycle, most of it drifting north into warmer water where eventually it melts. This annual pattern is quite unlike the wide-ranging life expectancy of a land-based glacier or an iceberg.

The global context

Here we focus on Antarctica's place in the world's environment, atmosphere and water systems. Some readers may already have asked themselves – or been challenged by friends about – how can they justify a trip to Antarctica? Clearly long-haul flights and cruising long distances in an engine-powered ship have a negative environmental impact. Personally I feel no eco-guilt: the greatest hazard is if people don't know, don't care about and don't understand Antarctic issues. I have yet to meet anybody who has visited who has failed to return with a different perspective on its place in the world.

The ozone hole

Antarctica's environment is globally unique, and, like the traditional canary in the coalmine, it acts as an early warning system. A good example of this was the British Antarctic Survey's discovery in 1985 of the 'ozone hole'. Ozone is a 3-atom form of oxygen formed naturally in the stratosphere by sunlight. It screens out ultraviolet radiation (UV-B and UV-C) that is harmful to all living creatures – from plankton and krill up to humans and Blue whales.

Blue highlights the ozone hole over Antarctica in 1999

A major cause of ozone depletion is the synthetic chemicals that were once widespread in refrigerators and aerosols. When they reach cold clouds in the stratosphere, they are broken down into chlorine by sunlight. Chlorine destroys ozone, thus creating an enormous hole which used to cover the entire continent in the spring (early October) and tends to be largest for a month from mid-September.

Happily once the stratosphere warms up over the summer, the clouds disappear and the ozone depletion ceases until the following spring. Less happily, the effect of the ozone hole on the marine ecosystem comes at a sensitive time of year for breeding cycles and growth. During the duration of the ozone hole, scientists found a 6% to 12% reduction in marine productivity.

Once the role of these CFCs (chlorofluorocarbons) was recognised, international negotiations led to their production being phased out under the Montreal Protocol (in force from 1989). The CFCs reached their maximum in 2006, and the ozone hole its maximum extent in 2017. Since then, its maximum size has been shrinking, although it still varies widely through the year. Early season visitors must be aware of the consequently greater risk of sunburn in October/November.

The hole is measured on 2 October each year, and recovery will take decades because the CFCs persist in the atmosphere. But the 20-year lag between recognising a problem, taking action and starting to see results underlines the value of an early warning system, as well as the need to remain vigilant.

Glaciers, ocean ice and sea levels

Antarctica is planet earth's reservoir. It holds captive about 30 million cubic km of ice, which is 90% of the planet's freshwater ice, the other 10% being shared among Greenland, the Arctic and high mountainous areas. This doesn't mean it holds 90% of the world's fresh water, because liquid water is also stored underground in aquifers and on the surface in lakes and rivers. But nearly 70% of all our water is stored in ice sheets, glaciers and permanent snow cover, meaning that over 60% of our fresh water is frozen into Antarctica.

A volume of 30 million cubic km is so enormous that it is hard to visualise. Imagine that all the Antarctic ice were to melt: that would raise global sea level by some 58 m/190 ft. That would clearly be catastrophic to human settlements, and at present it's just a thought experiment. However it does evoke the close link between Antarctic ice and the rest of the world. And if even a small percentage were to melt, hundreds of millions of people who live in the world's coastal towns and cities would be displaced.

Another factor is the temperature of the ocean. Like most liquids, water expands as it gets warmer, but only by a tiny amount, namely 0·021% for each degree Celsius. But a very small percentage of a huge volume is still significant, especially if compounded, year on year. The exact extent of the rise depends on the depth of the ocean at the point of measurement, but we can estimate using the NOAA global average depth of 3·7 km/ 12,100 ft. At that, each 1 °C rise in temperature would increase sea level by 77 cm/30 inches.

The thermal expansion effect is not large, then, but it is inexorable. Faster-moving factors include the melting of polar ice caps, the accelerated flow of glaciers into the ocean with faster calving, and the breaking up of ice shelves. All of these need to be monitored closely.

For cons, Antarctic glaciers were in a state of equilibrium: the mass of accumulating snow was balanced by the mass of snow transported downhill by glacier flow, so that the glacier mass remained constant. Since the 1950s, equilibrium has been disrupted by climate warming of up to 3° C (5·4 °F) around the Antarctic Peninsula. As a result, some glaciers have retreated or shrunk, and others have increased their downhill flow speed, leading to faster calving. Once calved, the ice melts much faster in water than on land: seawater conducts heat far better than land or air.

Albedo and positive feedback

When a glacier starts to melt, it triggers a positive feedback loop. *Albedo* (from the Latin word for whiteness) is a number that measures how well a surface absorbs or reflects solar energy (heat/light). A perfect absorber of solar energy would have zero albedo, whilst a perfect reflector would have an albedo of 1. The open ocean absorbs well, with albedo 0.06, deciduous woodland measures about 0·15 to 0·18 and bare soil typically about 0·2. The albedo of ice is much higher, ranging from 0·5 to 0·7, whereas fresh snow is higher still at about 0·8 to 0·9.

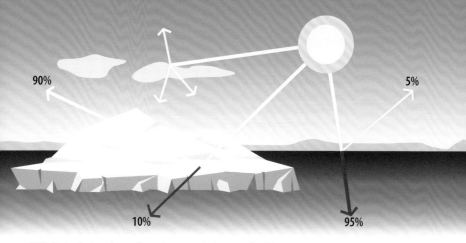

White high-albedo surfaces reflect solar energy, dark oceans absorb it

So the white, snowy surface of a glacier has high albedo, but as it retreats it reveals dark ground with much lower albedo. The ground absorbs more solar energy and heats up, causing the glacier to retreat further and faster. If the glacier is sliding into the sea and calving, the effect is stronger still. Not only is the open ocean an even better heat-absorber than bare ground, but also the ice melts faster in the sea than on land. Any reduction in albedo enters into a positive feedback loop that accelerates the warming process.

An international study of Antarctica's ice mass balance was published recently in *Nature*, reporting results gathered by 84 polar scientists working for 44 organisations. They used satellite data to track net changes in the mass of Antarctic ice between 1992 and 2017. They found a net loss of 2720 billion tonnes over the 25-year period, with the main losses coming from West Antarctica and also from the Peninsula, where the collapse of Larsen B and Wilkins ice shelves had triggered a sudden acceleration in the descent of local glaciers into the sea.

The loss of this mass of ice has raised global sea levels by 7·6 mm/0·3 ins. That may not sound like much, but about half of the increase happened in the final five years (2013-17) and the trend seems likely to continue. In fact, according to an article in *Nature Climate Change* published in late 2023, the accelerated melting of west Antarctica's ice sheet is now inevitable for the rest of the 21st century.

No matter how much carbon emissions are reduced or offset, even if the ambitious Paris Agreement to keep global warming below 1·5° C were to prevail, the rate of melting in West Antarctica will remain three times faster in the 21st century than it was in the 20th. If the West Antarctic ice sheet were lost completely, global sea levels would rise by 5 metres (over 16 feet) which would have a massive impact on low-lying settlements worldwide and the people displaced from them.

3 Discovery, exploration and exploitation

The history of Antarctica can be summarised under three headings: discovery, exploitation and exploration – albeit exploitation has arguably been continual. The timeline below indicates the dates in general, we list major explorations on pages 64-5 and the famous expeditions of Scott and Amundsen, Mawson and Shackleton are further described on pages 66 to 79.

1785	1840	1917
Discovery	Exploration	
Exploitation		

Terra Nova seen through an iceberg grott

Discovery

Aristotle had predicted the existence of a southern continent as long ago as 350 BC, and Ptolemy included it in a map of about AD 150. However these were just predictions based on an assumption that a counterweight was needed to 'balance' the land masses of the north. The French cartographer Finé was the first to label a huge circumpolar land mass as *Terra Australis*, whilst others called it *Terra Australis Incognita* (unknown land of the south).

In 1570 the Flemish cartographer Ortelius published his compendium atlas showing *Terra Australis* as by far the largest landmass, stretching north and into the tropics, see foot of page. Australia and New Zealand were unknown at the time, although Ortelius will have known of Magellan's circumnavigation of 1519-22. He called his huge continent *Terra Australis nondum cognita* or 'land of the south not yet known'.

Later maps show how this continent sometimes shrank, and sometimes disappeared altogether, until deeper exploration gradually reduced the area of guesswork. Even today, the mapping of coastal and frequently visited areas is far more detailed than the empty interior and huge expanses of east Antarctica. For an illustrated history of the mapping of Antarctica, see page 95.

Captain James Cook, on his second major voyage in 1773, crossed the Antarctic Circle three times and went south to 71° 10′ S but never sighted the continent, although two years later he discovered most of the islands in the chain that he named South Sandwich. Cook's description of abundant Fur seals on South Georgia in 1786 alerted the seal hunters. In 1819 Captain William Smith discovered the South Shetlands and landed on King George Island.

It wasn't until January 1820 that Prussian-born Fabian von Bellingshausen's ships first sighted the Antarctic mainland. Through thick snowfall they saw the Fimbul ice shelf, on the coast of Queen Maud Land at over 69° S: see the map on page 52. Sent by Czar Alexander 1 in the flagship *Vostok*, they had crossed the Antarctic Circle on 27 January 1820 and circumnavigated the continent, reaching a latitude of nearly 70° S. Other ships are believed to have sighted the continent later in the same year.

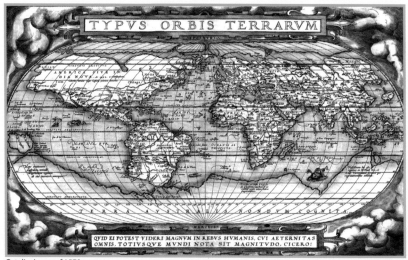

Ortelius' map of 1570

Contemporary engraving of a Weddell sealing expedition

Captain John Davis, an English-born American captain of the schooner *Cecilia*, made the first documented landing on the Peninsula on 7 February 1821. He put a boat ashore in Hughes Bay, near its north-west tip, and his log records 'I think this southern land to be a continent'. At this time the continent was still generally known as T*erra Australis*: it wasn't until the 1890s that Scottish cartographer John George Bartholomew coined the name *Antarctica*.

Scotsman James Weddell went on various sealing expeditions to the sub-Antarctic islands and Antarctica: on his 1823 voyage he went ashore on Saddell Island, South Orkney and collected six skins of a new species – later to be known as the Weddell seal. Having failed to find any harvestable sealing grounds, he turned south through the sea now named in his honour, and had unusually good weather. In fact he reached a record south of 74° 15′ S – some 530 miles/855 km inside the Antarctic Circle.

In 1839, another Scotsman James Clark Ross sailed from Hobart, Tasmania, in two ice-strengthened barques, *Erebus* and *Terror*. They managed to break through the pack ice, and were first to reach the Victoria Barrier (now known as the Ross Ice Shelf) and to land on Possession Island. His expedition lasted nearly five years and achieved a new record latitude of 78° 10′ S.

Exploitation of the seas and land

The wealth of wildlife in the Antarctic Ocean and sub-Antarctic islands led to more than two centuries of greedy and uncontrolled human exploitation. Cook's 1786 report from South Georgia triggered a stampede of Fur seal hunters. The main seal-hunting era lasted from about 1785 to 1890 and attracted over 1100 ships from all over the world.

The ships dropped off gangs of men on suitable beaches where they camped for months, killing seals and processing their corpses for pelts, seal meat and oil. The seals had no land predators so were easy targets. For the men, conditions were hard, but large fortunes were made by the owners after collecting and selling the produce. Long wooden clubs were the main method of brutal extermination.

Clubs being used to kill Fur seals

By 1823-24 sealing in the South Shetlands had become so excessive that Fur seals fell close to extinction. Numbers started to rally only in the 1950s, since when their recovery has been dramatic. In South Georgia alone, the population is estimated at 4 million, mainly on the north-western coast. In the breeding season, seals crowd some beaches so tightly that safe landings may be difficult or impossible.

Penguins, like seals, were easy targets for extermination: they are curious animals that had no experience of land predators until humans arrived. Penguins were killed brutally with clubs, mainly for their oil. Horrifically, some were boiled alive. The hunt for oil escalated remorselessly once ships were equipped to hunt whales. Whale slaughter began in 1904 when Captain Anton Larsen established Grytviken as a whaling station on South Georgia's best natural harbour. (In 1893 Larsen had been the first to ski on the ice shelf which was later named after him.)

The number of whales taken was modest at first, with the culling of 183 animals in 1904. However by 1912-13 the combination of land stations, factory ships and 62 hunting boats killed and processed nearly 11,000 whales. Floating factory ships were a particular menace because they evaded government limits, and by 1930-31 the annual kill had risen to about 40,000 and remained at that level for decades. Boiling strips of blubber created whale oil that could be sold for lighting, tanning leather, an ingredient in soap and margarine, and a lubricant.

As each species of whale was driven to the brink of extinction, the whalers switched to another species. By 1965 when whaling ceased on South Georgia, records show that a total of over 41,500 Blue whales and over 87,500 Fin whales had been killed since 1904, plus over 45,500 assorted Humpback, Right, Sei and Sperm whales.

Whales are now partly protected by the Southern Ocean Whaling Sanctuary that was set up in 1994 by the International Whaling Commission to protect the whales' main feeding grounds and allow recovery of endangered species. Of its 24 member nations, only Japan opposed it at the time, and until 2014 Japan's whaling fleet was allowed to catch up to 1000 Minke whales. The last attempt to ban whaling (in 2016) failed to reach the 75% majority needed and was opposed by Japan, Russia, Iceland and Norway.

Exploration timeline 1840-1917

Many expeditions set out from different countries between 1840 and 1917, most of them adventurous individual efforts. From 1895-1917, the Heroic Age of Exploration often had some support from scientific bodies or governments, but World War 1 brought a different perspective.

After the chronological list, we cover four expeditions in more detail: the race to the South Pole in 1911-12 by two teams – the British, led by Scott and the Norwegians, led by Amundsen. We tell the less famous story of Mawson's expedition in 1911-14, including his solo survival odyssey. Finally, we cover Shackleton's doomed attempt at a trans-Antarctic crossing, which history has reinvented as an epic success story after his rescue of the *Endurance* crew.

1840 The first Antarctic maps were drawn by a US expedition led by Charles Wilkes and British sealer William Smith, followed up by Edward Bransfield who claimed 'discovery'.

1841-2 James Clark Ross reached the world's southernmost point of open ocean, later named Bay of Whales by Shackleton (and used by Amundsen as his Ross Sea base).

1895 The Sixth International Geographical Congress was held at the Royal Geographical Society, London, to rekindle interest in Antarctic exploration.

1897 Adrien de Gerlache departed on the first major polar expedition aboard the *Belgica*, which was trapped in pack ice for 377 days. They endured great hardship and were the first explorers to overwinter inside the Antarctic Circle, eventually escaping the ice in March 1899. A young Norwegian called Roald Amundsen was among the crew.

1901-3 The Swedish Antarctic Expedition, led by geologist Nordenskjöld and skipper Larsen, explored Graham Land and brought back valuable samples. They survived terrible conditions and over-wintered twice on Snow Hill Island. They were stranded on Paulet Island from February to November 1903 after their ship *Antarctic* had sunk.

1902-3 Erich Drygalski led the German South Polar Expedition which named Kaiser Wilhelm II Land. When their ship *Gauss* was trapped in the ice, they started scientific work, ascending to 480 m in a tethered hydrogen balloon. After drilling and dynamite failed to release the ship, Drygalski laid a trail of dark ashes and rotting food waste. By reducing the ice's albedo (see page 59), this melted a 600 m channel leading to open water. However, it was a further two months before the ship escaped completely.

1901-4 The British National Antarctic Expedition was the first with the explicit goal of reaching the South Pole. Led by Robert Falcon Scott on *Discovery*, they cruised along the Ross Ice Shelf and set up winter quarters on Ross Island. In November 1902 Scott set off with Shackleton and Wilson, but their inexperience with skiing and sled-dog handling meant that they had to turn around at latitude 82° 16' 30" S.

1902-4 The Scottish National Antarctic Expedition, led by William Speirs Bruce, set off 'to reach as far south as is compatible with the best results to science'. They surveyed the South Orkney Islands and Weddell Sea on *Scotia*. Speirs was considered for a post on Scott's *Discovery* but organised his own expedition instead. His team set up Antarctica's first meteorological station, sold to Argentina in 1905; it has collected data continuously ever since. On return, Scotia made landfall at the Marine Biological Station at Millport, Firth of Clyde, where this memorial stands.

1903-5 French doctor Jean-Baptiste Charcot (1867-1936) led the French Antarctic Expedition in a ship that he funded personally; it explored the west coast of the Peninsula and discovered Port Lockroy and Port Charcot, the latter named for his father.

1908-9 Ernest Shackleton's *Nimrod* expedition (which included Mawson and Wild) climbed Mt Erebus (3794 m/12,450 ft) and believed that they had reached the magnetic South Pole: see page 71. Shackleton and three others narrowly failed to reach the geographic South Pole. To avoid death by starvation, Shackleton turned them around when only 112 miles/180 km short of the Pole, at 88° 23′ S: see the map on page 67.

1908 Charcot's second expedition in the newly built *Pourquoi Pas?* continued his earlier exploration, circled Adelaide Island and set up a shore station in the winter of 1909 to conduct research.

1911-12 Roald Amundsen and four other Norwegians reached the South Pole in December 1911. The next month, Robert F Scott and four team members also reached the Pole but all five died on the return journey: see the map on page 67 for both routes.

1911-14 Douglas Mawson, a Yorkshire-born Australian geologist, led the Australasian Antarctic Expedition to explore new areas west of Cape Adare and conduct research. Many people rate his survival from an ill-fated sledging trip as the most impressive solo survival story of all time.

1914-17 Shackleton's Imperial Trans-Antarctic Expedition was an ambitious plan to cross the continent via the Pole. Two ships, *Endurance* and *Aurora*, were needed, but there was no means of communication between the two. After *Endurance* was entrapped by ice, it drifted and sank. Shackleton's eventual rescue of the 22 men left on Elephant Island became famous; the deaths among the *Aurora* team have tended to be forgotten.

Shackleton's Nimrod Hut, Cape Royds, used in winter 1908

The race for the South Pole, 1911-12

Roald Amundsen (1872-1928) led the Norwegian team who were first to reach the South Pole on 14 December 1911. His winter Antarctic experience dated back to the *Belgica* trip in 1897-99 and he had also spent three winters in the Arctic, and was first to navigate its Northwest Passage (1903-6). During these expeditions he learned a great deal from the native Inuit about dog-handling, polar clothing and how best to travel on snow and ice.

When Amundsen sailed from Norway in August 1910, all but three of his team still thought that the goal was the North Pole. Only at Madeira did he reveal to his stunned crew that the goal had switched to the South Pole. He sent a disingenuous telegram to Scott: 'Beg leave to inform you Fram proceeding Antarctic'. His secret change of plan was triggered by two explorers, Cook and Peary, who claimed to have reached the North Pole (in 1908 and 1909), although probably these claims were false. The upshot was that Amundsen wanted to beat Scott to the South Pole instead, and felt that secrecy would help him to win the race.

Amundsen's expedition was methodically planned. His ship *Fram* had a diesel engine that made it more nimble than coal-fired steamships, and a rounded hull designed to rise above the pack ice, instead of being trapped. He took several backups of all critical items, carried spare food and fuel and laid ten well-marked depots extending to 82° S. The cached food stores amounted to 3400 kg and was crucial to their success, as were the 97 North Greenland dogs. He always intended the use of exhausted or dead dogs as food for the remaining dogs, and his team were all experienced skiers and dog-handlers.

He and four others set off on skis on 19 October 1911 from their base Framheim on the ice shelf at Bay of Whales. This had the advantage of being 100 km closer to the Pole than Scott's starting point, but they had to navigate a new route up to the polar plateau from the ice shelf. Each of four lightweight sledges was pulled by 13 dogs, saving the men's strength and reducing their food needs. They made good time, which reduced the pressure on food rations.

After climbing the Axel Heiberg Glacier, they crossed the polar plateau and arrived at the South Pole on 14 December, where they camped for three days, calculating their position carefully and making weather observations. Amundsen claimed the plateau for Norway and named it King Haakon VII Land, leaving a note for Scott in their green tent. When they returned to Framheim on 25 January, Amundsen reported that they still had 'two sledges and 11 dogs; men and animals all hale and hearty'.

The Fram under sail in the Southern Ocean

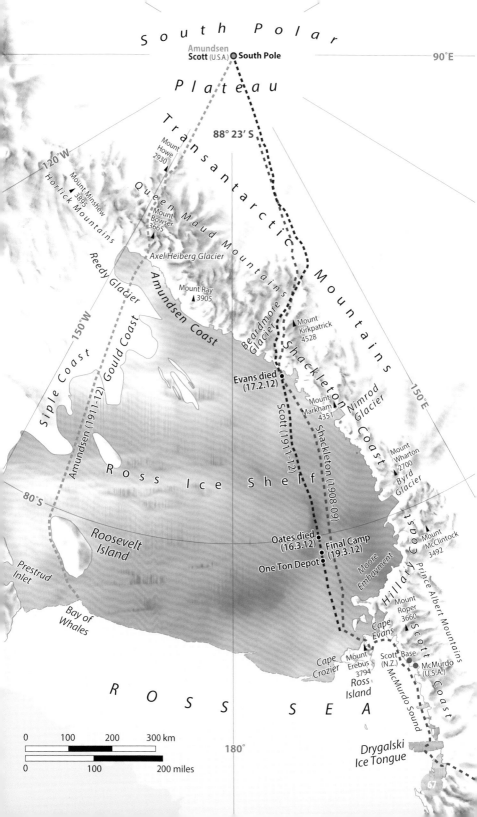

Like Amundsen, Robert Falcon Scott (1868-1912) was far from a novice: his *Discovery* expedition (1901-4) had been the first explicit attempt to reach the Pole. Although the three men turned around while still about 500 miles/800 km short, the whole experience was a great training ground and provided food for thought. Scott realised that their inexperience with skiing and dog-handling had been a limiting factor. However, it led him to experiment with motorised sledges and ponies rather than acquiring the skills of dog-handling and skiing.

Both Scott and Amundsen could have learned from Shackleton's near miss in 1909 when he had to turn his men around at 88° 23′ S to avoid death by starvation. He later told his wife Emily 'I thought you'd rather have a live donkey than a dead lion'. The deadly calorific calculus of man-hauling heavy loads in extreme cold was not then fully understood, but Shackleton's bold decision averted disaster.

To man-haul in extreme cold, humans need vastly more fuel than normal. On short rations, especially when man-hauling, they lack energy and become more vulnerable to cold, diseases, frostbite and sores. Losing muscle mass and with energy depleted, they go slower, which in turn means that more food is needed to cover the distance. When man-hauling, it's tempting to lighten the sled, because extra energy is needed to haul the added weight of further rations and fuel. Slow starvation leads to progressively slower progress, which accelerates the starvation.

Scott's British Antarctic Expedition had sailed from New Zealand on 29 November 1910 and arrived at Ross Island in *Terra Nova* in January. From their base at Cape Evans, they embarked on a depot-laying programme to support the journey to the Pole. After trying the motor-sledges, Siberian ponies and dogs, Scott settled upon man-hauling the sledges while walking or skiing – the most strenuous (and most calorie-consuming) exercise of all.

Captain R F Scott

On 24 October, only days after Amundsen, the polar journey began with 16 men, two motor sleds, 10 ponies, 23 dogs and 13 sleds. The plan was progressively to send back surplus people and animals until the final polar four-man team was chosen to go on alone. In practice the ponies were not a success and had to be shot on 9 December.

When two four-man teams reached latitude 87°34′S on 4 January 1912, they were still 150 miles (240 km) short of the Pole. Scott had already chosen Edward Wilson and two others, but the night before they left, he added 'Birdie' Bowers to make a five-man team and sent back the other three.

Given that the tent, skis and supplies had all been planned for a four-man team, this seems an astonishing decision. For all that Bowers was a good navigator, seemed impervious to the cold and appeared to have boundless energy, he was still another mouth to feed. His great strength as a sled-hauler was handicapped by his lack of skis, which had been cached earlier. In the mealtime photo opposite, taken by Oates, the team looks cheerful, oblivious to their impending death by slow starvation.

Crowded tent at mealtime: Evans, Bowers, Wilson and Scott

After great privations and hardship, Scott's team eventually reached the Pole on 17 January. They were devastated by the sight of the green tent with its Norwegian flag. They had been beaten by 35 days, and Scott's diary records 'The worst has happened … Great God! This is an awful place.' Much worse was to follow. A combination of starvation, appalling weather and ill health meant that none of them survived the return journey.

Evans died in a delirious sleep on 17 February. Over the next four weeks, the weather was unusually cold even by Antarctic standards, with temperatures below -40 °C (-40 °F). The team were managing shorter distances each day. Scott's diary records 'we know we cannot equal half our old marches, and that for that effort we expend nearly double the energy'.

'Titus' Oates was badly frost-bitten and so weak that he could not pull the sled at all, trudging beside it. Conscious of slowing the group, he prayed that he would never wake up. Having survived the night, on 16 March he calmly walked out into the raging blizzard, with the immortal understatement 'I am just going outside and may be some time'.

That left Scott, Bowers and Wilson, who continued a further 20 miles/32 km before making their final camp on 19 March. Their progress was slowed by extreme cold, which exacerbated their problems of hypothermia, food shortage and dehydration. Lack of fuel was a persistent issue, caused by the creeping of kerosene from its containers and perishing of the leather washers. Without fuel, they couldn't melt snow and would die of thirst.

There had been a tragic mixup over Scott's written orders to the dog driver Meares that a dog team with supplies should meet the Pole party at 82° S on 1 March to support their safe return. Later it emerged that, instead of the experienced navigator Wright, the young and extremely short-sighted Cherry-Garrard had been sent. Unable to navigate well, he had been told to go no further than One Ton Depot, within sight of Mount Erebus. This countermanded Scott's order for a team to meet them further south, which would have saved their lives.

Instead, a fierce blizzard pinned the three to their tent, agonisingly only 12·5 miles/20 km short of the supplies at One Ton Depot (79° 29' S). Over the next ten days, with supplies exhausted and storms raging outside the tent, they all wrote their letters of farewell. It appears that Scott was the last to die, probably on 29 or 30 March.

The search party of November 1912 found their bodies, their letters and notes, rolls of film and fossils (*Glossopteris*, from a 250 million year old beech-like tree) weighing some 16 kg that the team had been dragging on sleds. These fossils demonstrated that the continent was once forested and joined to other continents. They also show an extreme commitment to research: lesser (or saner?) mortals would have improved their own chances of survival by lightening their loads.

Scott was leading a team of officers, gentlemen and scientists with lofty twin goals – to be first to the Pole and to complete an ambitious programme of scientific research. He took ponies, but was unaware of how badly suited they were to the climate and the deep snow. He also took dogs but didn't invest in sled-dog training. His expedition was weighed down by its commitment to collecting samples of rocks and fossils.

Amundsen took men that could ski and dogs that could pull, with a clear plan that, if need be, the former could eat the latter. His single-minded focus on reaching the Pole first was combined with meticulous planning. His team travelled faster and earlier in the season than Scott's, when the weather was less hostile. They carried no excess weight, but plentiful rations helped them to stay stronger and healthier, on their return trip actually gaining weight. Scott's team never recovered its morale after the body-blow of losing the race, and their desperate lack of supplies defeated their starvation-weakened bodies.

Despite his famous success, Amundsen had also made mistakes: impatience led him to make a false start against advice on 8 September. Despite good progress at first, it soon became clear that the men were too cold to sleep at night, and the dogs were suffering terribly with frostbite. They left most of the equipment at a depot at 80° S to lighten their loads, but on the way home several dogs froze to death and others had to be carried on the sleds. Amundsen raced back to Framheim leaving behind some of his team members out on the ice without food or fuel. This understandabley led to criticism and discontent.

Amundsen's strategy relied heavily on dogs and dog meat

Mawson's expedition, 1911-14

Douglas Mawson, a Yorkshire-born Australian geologist, had been invited by Scott to join *Terra Nova* as its chief scientist. However, he decided instead to lead his own Australasian Antarctic Expedition to explore new areas west of Cape Adare and conduct research. He recruited a talented team including John King Davis, who had been chief officer and later captain of *Nimrod*, polar veteran Frank Wild (who had also declined Scott's invitation, seeing him as 'too much the Navy man') and Frank Hurley, from Sydney.

Hurley was a young self-taught photographer who had bought a Kodak Box Brownie at the age of 17. As soon as he heard of Mawson's plans, he offered his services for free. His brilliant images of Shackleton's expedition soon made him famous, as did his later photos and films from World War 2.

Mawson managed to buy *Aurora* for £6000, and his extensive refit included rigging and making space for laboratories. They sailed from Hobart in December 2011, and discovered what they named King George V Land. He set up his main base at Cape Denison, 300 miles/500 km west of Cape Adare, unaware that katabatic winds made it the windiest place on earth. 'Day after day the wind fluctuated between a gale and a hurricane' Mawson commented, and they recorded winds of up to 180 mph/290 kph.

Their proximity to the South Magnetic Pole made it an ideal location for researching the earth's magnetic field; Magnetograph House remains the best-preserved building at Cape Denison. Meanwhile, a team of eight led by Wild set up camp on the Shackleton Ice Shelf some 1500 miles/2400 km west of Cape Denison – much further away than intended because of problems finding a suitable landing. Over the next two seasons various sledging parties covered over 2500 miles/4000 km of hostile, virgin territory and *Aurora* navigated 1800 mile/2900 km of uncharted coastline.

Mackay, David and Mawson at the South Magnetic Pole (Nimrod Expedition 1909)

Dog team pulling a sled on the Australasian Antarctic Expedition

The expedition's many firsts included discovering and collecting the continent's first meteorite and maintaining radio contact with another continent (Australia) by means of their wireless relay station on Macquarie Island. Mawson had also acquired a small monoplane which they cannibalised to make a motorised sledge which did some successful load-hauling on the ice before it broke down.

The team spent two years on a systematic programme of biological, geological and oceanographic research so extensive that it took 30 years to complete publication of all the results. Frank Hurley later summarised it thus: 'Shackleton grafted science on to exploration – Mawson added exploring to science'.

The team made many dog-sledging trips to explore uncharted territory in King George V and Terre Adélie. Disaster struck the one into Oates Land that began on 10 November 1912. Mawson set out with British soldier Ninnis and Swiss mountaineer and expert skier Mertz. By 14 December they had covered 310 miles/500 km, but Ninnis disappeared down a deep crevasse taking with him dogs, a sledge carrying their tent, all the dog food and nearly all the food for humans.

Despite their search efforts, no trace was found and Mawson and Mertz reluctantly had to continue by man-hauling. With so little food of any kind, killing and eating the remaining dogs was their only option if they were to live long enough to complete the homeward trek. Sadly on January 7 Mertz died, famished and freezing, probably also poisoned by dog livers.

Mawson somehow limped on alone for a further 100 miles/160 km, enduring one of the most extreme survival challenges of all time – so severe as to provoke speculation from armchair explorers that he must have resorted to cannibalism. To understand why this is unfounded, read about Jarvis's re-enactment of Mawson's journey: see page 81. He makes a powerful case that Mawson did not need cannibalism, but that he showed exceptional mental and physical survival skills.

When Mawson staggered back into camp on 8 February, he was so emaciated and exhausted that the team failed to recognise him. He had lost an estimated 35 kg (77 pounds) of weight and his body was breaking down. He found that he had missed *Aurora* by hours, the ship having waited three weeks beyond its scheduled departure date. Contact was made and *Aurora* tried to return to collect them, but was prevented by a gale.

Hodgeman crawling back into the hut after collecting weather data (1913)

Mawson and the six men left as a rescue party then spent a further winter in the hut: see the photos opposite and below. They collected magnetic and meteorological data as best they could, but were largely hut-bound by extreme blizzards. Their ordeal finally ended when *Aurora* returned on 13 December and after 11 days they finally left Cape Denison. Even so, Mawson insisted on a coastal and seabed survey in January 2014, a decision that led to falling out with his sleep-deprived captain Davis.

After an arduous journey, the *Aurora* returned to Adelaide on 26 February 1914 to a heroic reception. Mawson married his fiancée on 31 March and they travelled to London where he visited Ninnis' parents, lectured to the Royal Geographical Society and accepted his knighthood from George V on 29 June.

After his return to Adelaide, Mawson had to settle the expedition's considerable debts. The government declined to buy *Aurora* for £15,000 so he sold it to Shackleton at a bargain £3200. He wrote his own account of the expedition *The Home of the Blizzard* and wanted to distribute Hurley's film of the same name, but there were contractual issues. The outbreak of war in 1914 delayed publication of his two-volume book and hampered his attempts to settle up. Mawson's work has been strangely neglected compared with the fame of Amundsen, Scott and Shackleton. To find out more about his achievements, see pages 94 and 95.

Mawson's main base hut, Cape Denison

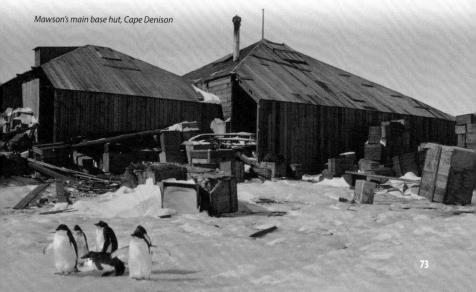

Shackleton's expedition, 1914-17

Shackleton's Imperial Trans-Antarctic Expedition had the very ambitious goal of a full continental crossing via the South Pole. He planned that *Endurance* would land a party from the Weddell Sea, while his second ship *Aurora* (bought from Mawson) would land from the Ross Sea. The latter was to place tons of supplies at five sites to a latitude of 83° S, in the hope that the *Endurance* party would locate them after passing the South Pole, and thus survive long enough to reach the Ross Sea.

Endurance was skippered by New Zealander Frank Worsley. They sailed from Plymouth on 8 August, spent some time in Buenos Aires for refitting, repairs and refuelling in mid-October and finally reached South Georgia on 5 November, far behind schedule. There they spent a month stowing provisions and refuelling with coal. The whalers had discouraging news of the extent of pack ice in the Weddell Sea and Shackleton realised that they would have to overwinter on the ice.

The ship finally left Grytviken on 5 December, heading for the Weddell Sea. Meanwhile his man Mackintosh was in Hobart trying to equip and find crew for *Aurora*. Shackleton had promised a meagre £1000 for the whole task and even that hadn't arrived, so hasty attempts to mortgage the ship were needed. Preparations were chaotic and *Aurora* finally left Hobart, undersupplied and weeks late, on Christmas Eve.

Mackintosh was worried that Shackleton's polar journey had already begun and was keen to start laying provisions for it. With no means of communication between the two teams, Shackleton's grandiose plan was doomed to fail. In fact they never came within 2000 miles of each other, and Mackintosh never knew that the *Endurance* party had postponed their start.

Progress in the Weddell Sea had been so slow that *Endurance* crossed the Antarctic Circle only on 30 December. Crucially, when they reached Glacier Bay on 15 January, Shackleton rejected Worsley's strong advice to make winter quarters in its sheltered harbour, insisting on the goal of the Vahsel Bay. Just four days later *Endurance* was entombed by the pack ice some 60 miles/100 km east of Vahsel Bay, never to escape until she sank. Frank Hurley's images of the ice-bound ship are dramatic.

Endurance then drifted north-west through uncharted waters, was crushed by the ice and Shackleton had to abandon ship on 27 October 1915. The ship finally sank four weeks later, on 21 November. Throughout this time, Worsley kept careful track of their location and found they had drifted some 550 miles (900 km) north of their furthest south position in February.

Endurance in the Weddell Sea

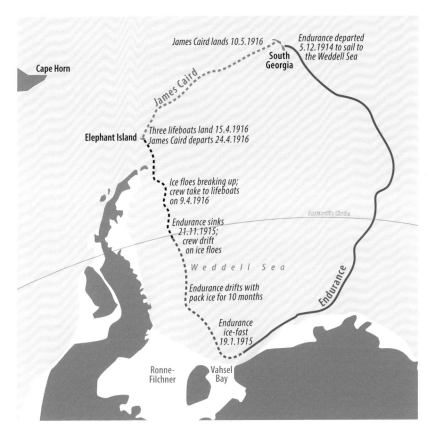

Over the many months of living on the pack ice, maintaining morale was perhaps Shackleton's greatest challenge, and he excelled at it. His plans for getting his men home alive had to change frequently with the changing state of the sea and the pack. His close advisers were polar veterans Frank Wild and Tom Crean, and skipper and navigator Frank Worsley.

On 23 March they gained their first clear sighting of land, but it was 60 miles to the west, across an impassable stretch of broken ice and sea. 'It might have been 600 miles for all the chance we had of reaching it' Shackleton wrote. Their ice floe, renamed Patience Camp, continued its northward drift apace. Their attention turned to Elephant Island, some 100 miles/160 km to the north: its shape resembles an elephant's head with trunk pointing east: see the map on page 76.

Meanwhile, supplies were running low, their ice floe was starting to break up under pressure and the Antarctic winter loomed. There was no alternative to shooting and eating the last of the dogs (on March 30). After a further ten days of anxiously watching the ice floes colliding and splitting alarmingly, on 9 April the Patience Camp floe split again, leaving the men with little more than standing room. Loading and launching the three lifeboats into the Weddell Sea suddenly became urgent.

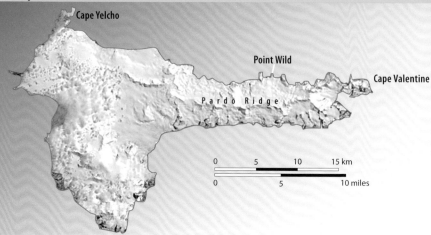

After various changes of plan forced by strong winds, currents and terrible weather, Shackleton's three lifeboats finally made landfall at Cape Valentine on the icy, windswept Elephant Island on 15 April 1916. Many of the men were in such poor condition that Wild said at least half of them would not have survived another 12 hours in the boats. It was 71 weeks since they had stood on dry land, and some of the men had to be carried or helped ashore, others were sobbing or laughing uncontrollably.

However, there was no safe camping site at that landfall, so next morning they had to get back into the boats to reach the place that Wild had discovered in a hasty scouting voyage. Now known as Point Wild, it lay 7 miles/11 km to the west, but it took the little boats six hours to complete this short journey in the gathering gale. Its advantages included a generous supply of Elephant seals and penguins, unlimited fresh water from the nearby glaciers and relative shelter from the ocean surges.

Shackleton knew that most of his 28 men would not survive a further trip in the Southern Ocean, and that Elephant Island was at best a short-term refuge. It was nowhere near where any search party might seek, no shipping lanes were nearby and there was no radio with which to seek rescue. Without action, their realistic chance of rescue was zero.

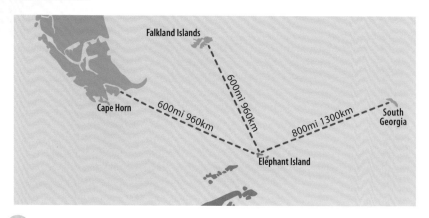

From Elephant Island, the nearest inhabited land was either Cape Horn or Port Stanley in the Falklands – both about 600 miles/960 km away: see the map.   But with strong westerly winds and currents, neither was attainable in a lifeboat with no engine. South Georgia was further away (800 miles/1300 km) but with careful navigation, just might offer a faint hope of landing and raising a rescue party.

So Shackleton and five carefully chosen men would attempt an epic voyage to South Georgia where there would be whaling stations. The *James Caird*, at 23 feet/7 m was not only the largest of the three lifeboats, she was also built more sturdily (double-ended and carvel-planked) with reserve buoyancy. Worsley had commissioned it specially for the *Endurance* (which had arrived with only two Norwegian lifeboats) and it was about to prove its value.

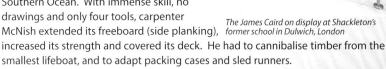

Shackleton had given evidence at the enquiry that followed the sinking of the Titanic in 1912. This led to the 1913 *Convention for Safety of Life at Sea* which improved standards for ships' lifeboats. The *James Caird* was the obvious choice, but it needed a major upgrade before attempting a long voyage in the hostile Southern Ocean. With immense skill, no drawings and only four tools, carpenter McNish extended its freeboard (side planking),

The James Caird on display at Shackleton's former school in Dulwich, London

increased its strength and covered its deck. He had to cannibalise timber from the smallest lifeboat, and to adapt packing cases and sled runners.

The six men set off on 24 April (Easter Monday) 1916, taking enough food and water to last them for a month, with compass, binoculars, and, for Worsley to navigate, a sextant. The sun's appearances were rare, and the huge waves meant that two men had to steady him while he aimed his sextant at the sun. That they found South Georgia after 16 days was testament to Worsley's incredibly accurate navigation. That the *James Caird* completed this voyage without capsizing reflected McNish's skilful modifications, as well as the seamanship of Worsley, Crean and others.

The crew endured terrible hardships on the voyage, suffering penetrating damp cold, tainted drinking water and severe storms.   Their clothing was for sledging, not seafaring, in layers of heavy wool, with gloves and boots made of reindeer skin. Approaching the island, they had to stand off because of a serious hurricane, eventually making landfall at King Haakon Bay in near-darkness on 10 May 1916: see the map on page 78. Only after making a fire with driftwood could they finally start to dry their clothes and sleeping bags.

The south-west coast of South Georgia has very few landing places and all the whaling stations were on the north-east coast. Three of the team were so exhausted that they had to be left behind at Peggotty Camp, sheltering under the upturned lifeboat, with carpenter McNish in charge.

Across South Georgia to Stromness (May 1916)

Meanwhile Shackleton (with his two strongest team members, Frank Worsley and the lionhearted Tom Crean) would soon set off on the challenging first-ever traverse of the island's unmapped interior. They travelled light, with no tent, a coil of rope and footwear with improvised 'hobnails' (brass screws) for grip on the ice.

They climbed over high mountain passes, crossed crevassed glaciers and navigated steep and broken terrain. In one place they used a daring glissade because down-climbing was too slow. They were lucky with the weather, relentless in their efforts, and trekked over 22 miles/35 km of hostile terrain to reach Stromness. (They thought, wrongly, that the much closer whaling station at Prince Olav Harbour would already have closed.)

Helped by a full moon, they set off at 3 am on May 19th and managed this prodigious feat in about 36 hours, virtually without sleep. Shackleton kept watch while the other two slept, but woke them after only 5 minutes, telling them that they had slept for half an hour to encourage them to keep moving. They finally staggered into Stromness, filthy and bedraggled, at about 4 pm on 20 May 1916.

They caused shock and even fear at the whaling station before managing to speak to the manager Thoralf Sørlle. Once he recognised Shackleton, he organised food, baths and clean clothes, and immediate helped to set up a rescue. Worsley heroically sacrificed his first night in a soft bed to join the 11-hour voyage on a steam whaler *Samson* and guide its final approach to Peggotty Camp. McNish, McCarthy and Vincent were collected safely, after completely failing to recognise Worsley, who was clean, shaven and in borrowed clothes.

Rescue efforts: Elephant Island and the Ross Sea party (1916-17)

Attempts to rescue the 22 men left on Elephant Island dominated the next three months. The onset of winter and its obstructive ice conditions defeated the first three expeditions, which had to turn around respectively within 75 miles, 20 miles and 100 miles because of lack of fuel and/or impenetrable pack ice. Finally, the Chilean navy allowed its coastguard Yelcho (which had assisted at a previous attempt) to set off with a volunteer crew of 23 under its skipper Luis Pardo.

The steamer was Clyde-built in 1906 for coastal waters, used mainly for servicing lighthouses. With no proper heating, no double hull and no radio, it was ill-suited to a mission to cross the Drake Passage, let alone to coping with pack ice. However, its late August departure meant that Antarctic spring was imminent and the ice was scattered when, on 30 August the fog lifted to reveal the mountains of Elephant Island.

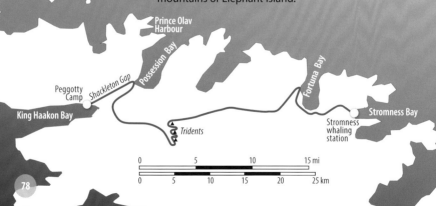

By noon they were at Point Wild, where to Shackleton's extreme relief all 22 men could be seen through binoculars, frantically waving and yelling. A small boat ferried Shackleton and Crean across the final 150 m to collect the men from the shore. There was a heavy sea and *Yelcho* urgently needed to escape the pack ice danger.

On the return voyage, Shackleton came to understand how well Wild had done to maintain morale, discipline and life itself among the 22 stranded men. With dwindling hope, limited food and a seemingly endless wait, rescue had arrived only just in time. They reached safety at Punta Arenas, Chile on 3 September 1916.

Meantime, the Ross Sea party had experienced terrible problems and poor leadership. A freak blizzard had torn their ship *Aurora* away from her moorings in May 2015, leaving the ten men marooned at McMurdo Sound with very limited supplies and equipment. Believing that the lives of Shackleton's party depended on laying supplies at the agreed five sites, they persevered despite the atrocious conditions of the Antarctic winter.

The group were under the dubious leadership of Mackintosh who had no previous experience of work on the ice. When he became unable to pull the sled, he was left behind with another invalid, sank into despair, and wrote letters of farewell. Meanwhile Joyce and two others tried to save the seriously ill Spencer-Smith, but on 9 March he died from scurvy, starvation and hypothermia.

Although Mackintosh and others recovered somewhat at the Discovery cabin (Hut Point), they were still cut off from base camp (Cape Evans) by miles of unstable sea ice. After seven weeks living in cramped squalor, on 8 May Mackintosh gambled on trying to cross the ice with Hayward, in the dark, despite strong warnings from the ice veteran Joyce. Neither man was seen again, presumed drowned, and Joyce assumed leadership of the remaining six men.

The poignant tragedy of the Ross Sea party was its pointlessness. Over six months they managed to cache 1800 kg of provisions by sledging some 1500 miles (2400 km) back and forth across the Barrier as far as 83° S. Far from approaching them across the continent via the Pole, Shackleton's men were by then drifting helplessly north on a disintegrating ice floe in the Weddell Sea. Had Shackleton been able to send the simplest of messages, all their efforts and sacrifices could have been avoided.

Strangely, after drifting for ten months the *Aurora* broke free from the ice with little damage, and made her way back to New Zealand. By December 2016 a government rescue had been organised and financed using *Aurora*. Shackleton (whose expedition funds had long been bankrupt) was allowed to join it only once he reluctantly accepted John King Davis as its commander.

On 10 January 1917 Shackleton was finally able to land near Cape Evans to collect the seven survivors of the Ross Sea party and hear about their two-year ordeal. He mounted a search for the bodies. After it was abandoned, he placed a message at their memorial cross overlooking Cape Evans.

By the end of 1919 Shackleton had published his book *South* – the story of his last expedition illustrated with photos by Hurley. The book was written by New Zealander Edward Saunders, the same journalist who had ghost-written his earlier book. The collaboration worked well: Shackleton dictated his memories and Saunders turned them into publishable prose. It has never been out of print since 1919.

The 20th and 21st centuries

Exploration continued after 1917, but the dark days of World War 1 had brought new priorities and sharp awareness of the costs of mounting rescue efforts for failed expeditions. In September 1921 Shackleton set off again in an ill-found ship *Quest* that skipper Worsley regarded as too small for Antarctic waters. Shackleton's heart condition had never been treated and in January 1922 he died of a massive heart attack in his cabin while anchored off South Georgia. Only 47 years old, he was eventually buried at Grytviken: the photo shows his gravestone with Polaris star. If you visit it, read his favourite Browning quotation on the back.

In 1929-31 Mawson returned to lead the British Australian and New Zealand Antarctic Research Expedition (BANZARE) which continued his comprehensive research programme. In 1954 Antarctica's first permanent scientific station was set up and named Mawson Station in his honour.

Exploration methods began to change as planes became more reliable. The very first powered flight was in November 1928 when Australian Hubert Wilkins with his US Army pilot Eielson flew above Deception Island for 20 minutes. After World War 2 ended, the US mounted Operation Highjump which sent 33 aircraft supported by 13 ships and 4700 men in 1946. This allowed aerial photography of about 75% of the continent's coastline.

The image of Antarctic explorers remained entirely masculine until 1947 when the first two women, Edith 'Jackie' Ronne and Jennie Darlington, were active members of the Ronne Expedition which flew over 250,000 square miles of unexplored coast, taking 14,000 photos. They overwintered, along with their husbands, on Stonington Island.

In 1955-58 Shackleton's grand ambition was finally achieved by the Commonwealth Trans-Antarctic Expedition (CTAE). The Crossing Party was led by British geologist and explorer Vivian Fuchs. Ed Hillary (of 1953 Everest fame) led the Ross Sea Party who supported them, setting up the Scott Base on McMurdo Sound and using Sno-Cat tractors to lay supply depots. The UK team took 99 days to cross the continent over 2158 miles (3473 km), collecting scientific data as they went.

Sno-Cat tractors in use on the CTAE

The Vinson Massif was discovered only in 1958 by a US Navy aircraft, and its summit Mount Vinson (4892 m/16,050 ft) was first climbed in 1966 by a private US expedition led by Nicholas Clinch. It is nowadays a well established challenge on the Seven Summits list, and at least 1200 climbers have summited with no deaths (so far), but many cases of frostbite.

Scientific work, especially geology, oceanography and climatology, became the main focus of Antarctic teams, notably from 1959 onwards. Advances in technology have transformed research methods: for example the sampling of deep ice cores to travel back in time to analyse the air composition, the use of satellite tracking devices on migrating whales, the use of drones to survey uncharted areas and the control of unmanned vehicles to explore the seabed.

Historic explorations recreated

A fascinating insight into the Heroic Age has been contributed by Tim Jarvis's life and work. Jarvis was born in Manchester in 1966 but has lived in Australia since 1997 as an environmental scientist and explorer. His many expeditions defy summary, but his strong theme is that he prefers to go unsupported. One example was his 1999 Antarctic journey, during which he reached the South Pole in only 47 days, faster than any previous unsupported team.

Jarvis has paid tribute to two legendary explorers by recreating their experiences. In 2007 he re-enacted Mawson's 1913 epic journey wearing authentic clothing and subsisting on similar starvation rations, losing some 18 kg (40 pounds) of body weight during the ordeal. His re-enactment was scrupulous, to the extent of 'falling' down and climbing out of a crevasse twice over, on the grounds that Mawson (whose fall was accidental) managed to climb out only at his second attempt. His book *Mawson: Life and Death in the Antarctic* tells this story compellingly and honestly: see page 94.

Jarvis's friendship with Alexandra Shackleton, grand-daughter of the great Ernest, eventually led to an even more ambitious recreation: the double challenge of the voyage from Elephant Island to South Georgia followed by the mountainous crossing to Stromness. He used a faithful replica of the *James Caird* with authentic navigation equipment of the era, and wore contemporary clothing. He completed this extraordinary feat in 2013 and, like his Mawson journey, turned it into a captivating and thoughtful book *Chasing Shackleton*: see page 94.

Jarvis on his 2013 traverse of South Georgia

Jarvis's was not the first reprise of the Shackleton crossing of South Georgia. In particular Stephen Venables has repeated it four times, including with Reinhold Messner and Conrad Anker for the IMAX film, *Shackleton's Antarctic Adventure*. Venables commented: 'we took about the same time [as Shackleton], 36 hours, but in our case spread over three days, with the luxury of being able to stop and pitch a tent at night … We found the Crean glacier a hideous maze of open crevasses'. Messner, who had fractured his foot leaping a huge crevasse, had stoically completed the trek, and commented: 'Shackleton's *Endurance* expedition was the greatest adventure … not only of the last century, it was the greatest adventure ever'.

The *Endurance* story finally came full circle in 2022 when marine archaeologist Mensun Bound made his second voyage to try to locate the wreck. He directed explorations on the *Agulhas II*, and the mission was a dramatic success. A large team searched the Weddell Sea in the general area where Worsley reported it to have sunk on 21 November 1915. Despite heavy sea ice and hostile weather, the wreck was finally located on the seabed at a depth of 3008 metres (1·9 miles). The search used state-of-the-art autonomous underwater unmanned vehicles – a gripping story told in Bound's book *The Ship beneath the Ice*: see page 94.

'This is by far the finest wooden shipwreck I have ever seen. It is upright, well proud of the seabed, intact, and in a brilliant state of preservation' said Bound. Despite the lapse of over a century since it sank, the *Endurance* looks eerily recognisable, its name and Polaris star clearly visible. The fact that it was only 4·7 miles/7·6 km from Worsley's reported sinking position is a tribute to his navigation, as well as to the search. Fittingly, the date of discovery was 5 March 2022, the 100th anniversary of Shackleton's burial at Grytviken, South Georgia.

Stern of Endurance photographed in February 2022 on the seabed at 3008 m

Antarctic claims, the 1959 Treaty and Madrid Protocol

Seven nations have laid claim to parts of Antarctica; Argentina, Australia, Chile, France, New Zealand, Norway and the UK. All these claims are of 20th century origin and none is currently being actively pursued because these countries are all signatories to the Antarctic Treaty of 1959.

Argentina and Chile, both former colonies of Spain, consider that they have inherited rights derived from a Spanish claim made in 1539. King Charles 1 of Spain (Emperor Charles V) granted a governorship to a merchant Pedro Sanchez de la Hoy over all lands south of the Straits of Magellan. The grant was intended to refer to Terra del Fuego and islands around Cape Horn but potentially it also related to the entire continent of Antarctica. Charles's right to do this rested on an even older document, the Treaty of Tordesillas of 1494.

Pope Alexander VI brokered this agreement between Spain and Portugal, both of which were making territorial claims in various parts of the world, based on the discoveries of sailors such as Christopher Columbus and Vasco da Gama. The Pope drew a line stretching north/south through the Atlantic near to the Azores. Spain was entitled to claim all new territories west of the line and Portugal all those to the east. Chile and Argentina maintain that, at the time, the Papacy was the legitimate arbiter on such matters and that the treaty, therefore, is still valid.

Apart from the South American claims, the oldest is that of France. In 1840 Jules Dumont d'Urville discovered the coast of Adélie Land, named it after his wife and claimed it for France. This claim was recognised by the UK in return for agreement about the boundary between British (now Australian) and French territory.

British and Norwegian interests date back to the Heroic Age of Exploration: see page 64. The UK laid claim to South Georgia, the South Sandwich and other islands in 1908, and extended this claim as far as the South Pole in 1917. When Britain ceased to claim any authority over Australia and New Zealand in 1931, part of the British claim passed to Australia. Similarly, Britain's 1841 claim to the Ross Dependency had already passed to New Zealand in 1923.

Norway had important whaling interests and sought to protect these by claiming Peter I Island in 1931. For similar reasons, Norway asserted sovereignty over Queen Maud Land in 1939. Britain and Norway agreed on the boundaries between their claims shortly after World War 2.

By then the USA was showing a keen interest and it undertook a major expedition in 1946/47 and established two large bases. Opinion had started to move away from the traditional type of colonial claim. In 1948 discussions began among the 7 claimants and the US with a view to establishing international joint ownership, but these came to nothing. However, based on their activity in Antarctica during the International Geophysical Year 1957/58, 12 countries, including the USA and USSR, agreed and signed the Antarctic Treaty in 1959.

The treaty defines Antarctica as all land and ice shelves south of 60° of latitude. It asserts that the primary interest is scientific and it bans military activity. It does not affect pre-existing claims, but seeks to prevent future claims. By 2023, 44 further countries had acceded, of which 17 have been recognised as conducting 'substantial research activity there' making a total of 29 countries that are full Antarctic Treaty Consultative Parties (ATCPs) which take part in decision-making by consensus. The other 27 are invited to the annual meetings in late May, but are non-consultative i.e. observers. The 12 founder ATCPs are Argentina, Australia, Belgium, Chile, France, Japan, New Zealand, Norway, Russia, South Africa, the UK and the US.

Over time, the original treaty has been extended into a wider Antarctic Treaty System. An important stage was the adoption of the Madrid Protocol on Environmental Protection in 1991/92. This was a commitment to 'the comprehensive protection of the Antarctic environment and … to designate Antarctica as a natural reserve, devoted to peace and science'. The Protocol specifically prohibits 'any activity relating to mineral resources, other than scientific research'. This and other key documents are available online from the official website **ats.aq**.

However, the Treaty includes provision for its own review after 50 years. 'If, after the expiration of 50 years any of the Antarctic Treaty Consultative Parties so requests, a conference shall be held as soon as practicable to review the operation of this Protocol'. This means that as soon as 2048 the ATCPs could revise or reject the anti-mining regulation and start stripping Antarctica of its mineral resources. This would create serious dangers, especially if new technologies such as drones, drilling and underwater prospecting were deployed in pursuit of mineral wealth. The future of the continent is uncertain.

The ATCPs comprise 12 founder countries (innermost circle) and 17 later ones (middle circle); outer circle countries are observers

Attempts at settlement in Antarctica

The long-standing rivalry between Argentina and Chile has resulted in bizarre attempts to establish permanent settlements in this ultra-hostile environment. In 1977, the Chilean President Pinochet visited Antarctica as part of trying to assert dominance. Argentina responded by flying the pregnant Silvia Morello de Palma, wife of the Esperanza research station's commander, to the station: see page 7 for its location. Her son Emilio was born there in January 1978 – Antarctica's first baby and part of Argentina's attempt to bolster its claims. The Argentine government passed a law banning the publication of any maps of Argentina that do not include Antarctica.

Major expansion has been under way in Esperanza since 1978, where at least seven more children have been born. The 2010 census claimed it had 66 inhabitants, and its 40-plus red buildings include a chapel, bank, post office, hospital, and school as well as chalets for ten families. It also hosts an ice runway, a gravel football field, graveyard and a small museum with relics from the Swedish expedition of 1903. Three explorers were stranded here after their ship was crushed by ice, and somehow survived the winter on seal meat. About 1100 tourists from cruise ships visit Esperanza each season. Its claim to be a scientific centre is undermined by its very limited laboratory capacity, most personnel being military with a minority of spouses and children.

It is not clear, however, that Esperanza is a permanent settlement. Its motto means 'permanence, an act of sacrifice' and it appears to be inhabited in rotation, with families serving a term of 12-14 months before returning to Argentina. Argentina's claim that their province of Tierra del Fuego extends 1000 km across the Drake Passage into Antarctica is quite a stretch.

Meantime Chile started sending recently married couples to one of its own Antarctic bases in order to provide babies that had been both conceived and born in the territory. Juan Pablo Camacho Martino was born at a Chilean base in 1984. By 2009, 11 children had been born in Antarctica, eight Argentinian and three Chilean. Whether these attempts to use babies and children to stake territorial claims will impress other countries is doubtful.

Claims to the Falklands

The Falkland Islands are claimed by both the UK and Argentina. This led to war as recently as April 1982 when General Galtieri's Argentine invasion force took control of the islands but was expelled 11 weeks later by a British naval expedition. A total of 635 Argentines, 255 Britons and three Falkland civilians died in the fighting, and some 25,000 landmines are part of its legacy. Many of these are still unexploded and dangerous to humans, but happily the penguins are not heavy enough to detonate them, and penguins have returned in force.

Indigenous people from the South American mainland may possibly have discovered or settled on the islands in prehistoric times but there is no evidence. Claims rest on the activities of Europeans over the last 500 years or so. The first confirmed landing was by John Strong, an English sailor in 1690.

However, no Europeans settled until a French expedition arrived in 1764. They quickly transferred their claim to Spain which maintained a small settlement until the early C19th. When Argentina became independent of Spain following the war of 1816-18, the islands were uninhabited. However, Argentina tried to maintain the Spanish claim until a British expedition took control in 1833.

Possession of the Falklands remains contested. Argentina continues to refer to them as Las Malvinas in maps, road signs and billboards and claims that, along with South Georgia and the South Sandwich Islands, they are theirs. The Spanish occupancy claim was based on in the late 18th and early 19th centuries and, following independence, Argentina believes it inherited the claim. They argue that the British occupied the islands illegally in 1833.

Britain, by contrast, dates its claim from its first landing in 1690 and de facto sovereignty since 1833. After 1840, immigration was encouraged and taken up mainly by Scottish settlers. The Falkland population is mainly of British descent, the official language is English and in 2013, 1513 of the 1517 residents who voted in a referendum wanted it to remain a British Overseas Territory.

Whilst Argentina argues that geographical proximity strengthens its claim, Falklanders consider themselves culturally and linguistically more British than Argentinian. They may be geographically much further from London (7850 miles) than Buenos Aires (1180 miles) – 12,630 km cf 1900 km – but 99·7% voted to remain British.

Police HQ in Stanley, Falklands

4 Practical information

Time zone and currency

An Antarctic ship normally takes its time zone from the port of departure, and may maintain that throughout your cruise. For example, Argentinian time is 3 hours behind Greenwich Mean Time (GMT/UTC) year-round, and this may apply on board throughout Antarctic sailings. However South Georgia is only 2 hours behind GMT and the ship's clocks may change to align with this, to avoid confusion in marine communications. Chilean time is 3 hours behind GMT in austral summer only, and 4 hours behind from April to October.

The currency used on board usually reflects the nationality of the ship, very seldom its departure port. Given high rates of inflation in South America, virtually all ships operate in either US dollars or euros, and extras will be added to your cabin bill for settlement typically on your last evening. Dollars are generally useful in South America too, but since ships operated by European companies use euros, keep this in mind when deciding how to carry cash. Cash is useful for tips and as backup to credit/debit cards: whenever internet connection is flaky, contactless transactions may fail.

What to pack

Read this well before departure, because most people want to buy at least some items specially for their trip. Don't go mad buying new stuff until you've read the section on weight restrictions. However if you don't already own suitable binoculars, read page 88.

Don't be misled by generous weight limits on international flights, such as 23 kg (50 lb) for hold baggage plus hand baggage. What matters is the stricter limit on internal flights to Ushuaia, which is typically 15 kg for hold (checked) baggage and 5-8 kg for carry-on bags. For flights from Chile to Antarctica, the limits may be stricter still. Excess baggage may be expensive (Argentina/Chile) or prohibited (Antarctica), so check exact limits before you pack. Minimise weight by taking small quantities, especially of toiletries, and garments that you can hand-wash.

All ships provide customers with rubber boots for reasons of biosecurity, so the only footwear that you need is for use in transit and on board. Choose shoes with good grippy soles in case of rough weather and wet, slippery decks. Most ships also supply their own brand of waterproof jacket (parka) which may be warmly lined: find this out before you pack. The ship's interior will be heated to a comfortable temperature and you can wear the jacket on deck as well as in the Zodiacs and ashore.

The dress code on Antarctic ships is informal, and on expedition ships very informal, so leave evening wear behind unless it's important to you to dress up and you are sure that it will be appropriate. For daytime clothing, the priority is to ensure compatible layers so you can adjust to different levels of wind chill, and to ensure that your outer layer is fully waterproof to protect you against sea spray, sleet and snow. Even if the ship provides a jacket and rubber boots, you still need waterproof trousers and some face protection e.g. sunglasses and/or goggles, and headgear such as a balaclava, neck gaiter and/or warm hat that you can fasten safely.

You will need different layers for different types of excursion, and for different weather. You may be far too warm on a land excursion when hiking uphill in still weather, whereas sitting on a fast-moving Zodiac for hours will require extra layers because the Zodiac's motion adds to the wind chill. You will need different layers at different times, and some kind of backpack or dry bag to store any layers that you aren't wearing. You may need several pairs of gloves, especially if you will be using a camera or smartphone. Fishing gloves with finger- and thumb-tips that flip up work well for some people, much warmer than having to take gloves off.

Among the heaviest items may be photographic gear, binoculars and whatever you need to occupy yourself for long flights and airport downtime, e.g. books, laptop and/or tablet and smartphone. Digital cameras are useless without well-charged batteries and memory cards. Read page 93 and consider taking a backup camera.

Unless you own good binoculars, consider buying or borrowing some for viewing the wildlife. The most important factors are the brightness of the image and a wide field of view: avoid a high degree of magnification which makes them hard to use on a moving ship. When looking for whales, used your naked eye to scan for the blow first, then, once located, raise the binoculars for a closer view. When on land near seals and penguins, having binoculars helps to give a great view without approaching the animals too closely.

Pack all of the above as hand baggage: cold and condensation can ruin delicate electronics and rough handling can damage binoculars. In any case, the lithium batteries that drive most digital cameras are not allowed in the aircraft hold. Be sure to check what type of power socket will be available on board ship and bring at least one suitable adapter. The voltage and pins may differ from both your home sockets and those in Chile/Argentina.

Many or most ships offer internet access depending on satellite visibility: see page 18. Sometimes it will be better to enjoy the moment rather than to stress about failing to update your social media. Manage expectations back home about how often you will be in contact. Having said that, you may wish to consider taking a tablet or laptop as well as a smartphone: you may want to enjoy and perhaps edit your photos on a larger screen.

Think twice before packing any heavy books, for example guides to wildlife: nearly all ships have a library on board and photographic books tend to be heavy. Since ebooks add no weight to a reading device, there is no need to run short of reading matter.

Take a generous supply of any medications that you need and pack them in your hand baggage, obviously. Sun protection is needed even on apparently dull days when the ultraviolet radiation is still intense: it is reflected from the ice, snow and water. Read page 57 about the ozone hole and be especially careful in early season. At minimum, you need polarising sunglasses or goggles, and high SPF lip balm and sun block.

Remember that flight connections and distances mean that journeys to and from Ushuaia will include several overnights. Coming from the northern hemisphere that involves somewhere much hotter that the weather you left behind. Buenos Aires is at latitude 35° S and its summer temperatures typically rise to at least 20-35 °C (68-95 °F), higher in a heat wave. Santiago de Chile is at 33·5° S and its climate more Mediterranean, with temperatures typically about 15-35 °C (59-95 °F).

When travelling in a group, hold (checked) baggage often has to be finalised the night before departure, so hand baggage may need to allow room for some overnight essentials, toiletries and medicines. This may apply also to the night before departure from the ship.

Passengers landing at a South Georgia beach

Before and during landings

Before landing in an area, and perhaps before every landing, you will be expected to clean your clothing and equipment for reasons of biosecurity: see page 31. You will be supervised and reminded, if need be, before approaching the boarding area for Zodiacs. You will always walk your rubber boots through a footbath before and after the Zodiacs. Never take anything edible ashore with you.

There are no toilet facilities on land, so if the landing is likely to be protracted or you have a weak bladder, take obvious precautions. Avoid drinking much beforehand, especially caffeine-laden or alcoholic drinks whose diuretic effects persist for many hours. Throat sweets can relieve a dry throat without drinking water. Although the crew will take a passenger back to the ship if need be, this interruption of precious time ashore will be unwelcome. If you are on an extended hike, you may need to take a pee bottle. However, for an overnight trip to camp on the ice, expect portable toilet facilities to be landed and removed next morning, so as to leave no trace.

All IAATO operators follow and must enforce its code of conduct about visitor behaviour during landings. Again follow the briefings, but generally this means keep to the path, observe any boundary flags that are in place, and never approach an animal more closely than 5 metres/16 feet. In some cases, you will be told to stay at least 15 metres/50 feet away.

Even 15 m could be too close: keep assessing whether the animal is reacting to your advance – if so, stop and back off. Conversely, if you keep still, a curious penguin may come right up to you and perhaps walk over your boots: that is both acceptable and enjoyable, as long as it's the animal that decides, not the human*. But don't get too close to a Fur seal or you risk a nasty, bacteria-laden bite. And an Elephant seal bull, because of its massive weight, could accidentally kill you without even noticing.

If one of your fellow passengers gets carried away and starts to approach an animal too closely in defiance of guidelines, this can endanger the landing permissions for everybody on your ship. Consider drawing it to the attention of one of the naturalists.

Adélie checks on a boundary flag

* not permitted while the 2023 avian flu rules apply, see imprint page.

Motion sickness

This section offers advice on prevention and management of seasickness. Fear of the Southern Ocean puts some people off the whole idea of an Antarctic cruise. Your choice of ship and cabin (see below) may help: modern cruise ships have stabilisers of various kinds, such as active fins with adjustable angles and anti-roll tanks. An ice-strengthened ship cannot have fins or anything else projecting from its hull, so its journey across the Drake Passage will be less comfortable than a large cruise ship.

In general, small ships are going to be tossed around in heavy seas more than larger, heavier ones, but some people find the slower movements on large ships harder to tolerate. There is no size or design of ship that will prevent seasickness in heavy seas if you are prone to it. Every individual is different and needs to find out for themselves how to cope. Some people are highly suggestible, and research has found that people may become seasick merely by expecting to be. If you are susceptible, take precautions, read this section carefully and, above all, try out any remedies long before your cruise departs.

The symptoms include dizziness, nausea, vomiting, sweating and feeling cold – very unpleasant while they last, albeit recovery is usually fast once the motion calms down. However the prospect of a two-day crossing of the Drake Passage may be daunting enough to make some consider flying in at least one direction: see page 26. Once on a cruise, take any medications as soon as rough weather has been announced: don't wait until you feel unwell or it may be too late.

The cause of motion sickness is the conflict between signals that your brain receives from various sources: your eyes, inner ear and muscles and joints. You can reduce or relieve the symptoms in various ways: for example reduce the extent of motion by your position on the boat, look at the horizon, seek fresh air on deck and consider taking or wearing various remedies.

To reduce the amount of motion that you experience, stay amidships, rather than going to the bow or stern, and also try to stay low in the ship rather than near its top deck. Aim to book a cabin on a low deck amidships, with at least a decent-sized porthole or window so that you can see out. For fresh air while awake, of course you need to ascend to deck level, and it may help to stand, not sit, so that your whole body is feeling and counteracting the ship's motion. Always look at the horizon or another distant point, never at the waves or anything moving nearby.

If feeling queasy, avoid making things worse by looking at any kind of screen or trying to read. If seriously unwell you may prefer to stay away from the sight and smell of food, perhaps fasting completely until you feel better, and if you can take a nap, that may help. But keep up your fluid intake, especially if you have been vomiting, to avoid dehydration. And if you do eat, snack on small amounts of bland food, avoiding rich or spicy foods, alcohol and caffeine.

Research has shown that ginger can help to overcome nausea, probably because it neutralises the receptor that plays a role in vomiting. So drink ginger tea or ginger ale, eat a ginger biscuit or take powdered ginger root in a capsule. Stay away from people who are talking about seasickness or suffering from it, lest the power of suggestion makes you ill.

Various medicines can prevent or reduce seasickness, but before you rush to the pharmacy or your doctor, consider two drug-free options. The first is wristbands that hold a small plastic bead against an acupressure point (called P6, Neiguan or Neikuan) on the inside of each wrist. This option doesn't work for everybody, but since wrist-bands are very cheap and free of any side-effects there is no harm in trying them. Some people believe in them totally, and that may explain why they work so well – when they do.

Several research studies have followed up anecdotal evidence that World War 2 navy recruits used controlled breathing to combat motion sickness and these results are impressive. Slow, deep breathing (6-8 breaths per minute, using your diaphragm) is known to increase parasympathetic nervous system activity. This is effective in reducing motion sickness, and has been reported in several carefully controlled studies. The effect may be stronger if you create a breathing rhythm that is out of sync with the ship's motion.

Two main types of drugs are used to treat motion sickness: antihistamines and scopolamine. The anti-nausea antihistamines will make you feel sleepy. Promethazine (also known by trade names Avomine, Phenergan or Sominex) is effective but has side-effects: as well as drowsiness, it increases your sensitivity to ultraviolet rays, already a hazard in Antarctica. In many countries it's on prescription for these reasons. Cinnarizine is another antihistamine, known by the brand name Stugeron. It blocks histamine from binding to receptors in the vomiting centre of the brain, and also improves blood flow in the inner ear. However it too is likely to make you drowsy and may have more serious side-effects.

Scopolamine is widely used to treat motion sickness by another method. Its active ingredient is hyoscine hydrobromide which blocks acetylcholine, a chemical found naturally in parts of your brain and central nervous system. Taken in tablet form, it can start working inside an hour. Scopoderm patches (worn behind the ears) allow a slow release and take up to six hours to work fully. Common side-effects include constipation, drowsiness, dizziness and a dry mouth, but disturbances of vision also occur.

On one cruise I met someone whose dizziness and blurred vision was so serious that and she had taken to her cabin. After a trip to the ship's doctor, she hastened to remove the Scopoderm patch. However, her symptoms persisted for a further 12-24 hours and she was unable to take part in landings, meals or lectures for several days. If you intend to use any drug, the advice is (a) read about its side-effects first, (b) try it out before you need to take it in earnest, and (c) at sea, take it early so your system can absorb it in time.

People have different genetic susceptibility to motion sickness, and factors such as age, gender and exposure also matter. Children are most at risk from about age 6 to 9 years. The risk then steadily declines through late childhood and teen years. Females are a bit more susceptible than males, and elderly people are least at risk.

Almost everybody experiences habituation: repeated exposure to disconcerting motion reduces the problem, which is why professional cruise staff are seldom seasick unless inexperienced or exposed to extreme conditions. However, if you have had such bad motion sickness that you have always avoided being at sea, your system has had no chance to habituate, and you are more at risk.

An entirely harmless symptom, disconcerting if you've never had it before, is motion after-effect: you may feel as if you are 'still at sea' long after your cruise ends. It doesn't affect everybody, but it may persist for days or even weeks on dry land. It does not bring nausea, and merely feels odd.

The Drake Passage in a Force 9 gale

Twelve tips on photography

Serious photographers will already have their techniques and systems, and have invested in suitable equipment. The advice below is for others, who may also want to consider relying on whatever images the ship's professional may offer for sale.

1 Consider composition before you take each shot: aim for strong foreground interest and try to avoid background clutter. When shooting from a moving ship or Zodiac, don't completely fill the frame because you may need room to correct a sloping horizon later.

2 Some people are content to rely on their smartphone, but many will achieve better results from a real camera: a viewfinder allows accurate framing, even in bright light. If you buy a camera specially for this trip, do so well in advance and invest time in learning how to use its controls with confidence.

3 The best camera is not the most expensive one, it's the one that you know how to use and which you carry with you whenever you need it. For many, that may mean sticking to your smartphone as a camera, despite its limitations for wildlife.

4 If you use a camera on automatic exposure, it will try to make everything look mid-grey, including snow and icebergs. To make them look white, learn how to override exposure. Cameras often have a button or menu that lets you dial in more light (plus sign) to make the subject lighter, or to reduce it (minus sign) to make it darker. If in doubt, 'bracket' the exposure, i.e. take two more versions with plus or minus values.

5 Rules about keeping your distance from wildlife mean that even for relatively large wildlife such as seals, you will get better results from a camera with a telephoto lens. Most smartphones are very competent at wide-angle shots, few are any good at telephoto. Digital zoom merely enlarges a small portion of the original image. Optical zoom gives higher resolution.

6 A 'bridge' camera (one with a fixed lens and a wide-range zoom) works well for many. Even if your camera body takes interchangeable lenses, conditions will be hostile and lens-changing is distracting. It may be better instead to take two bodies, each with a different range of zoom lens. This also provides backup in case of electronic failure.

7 Low temperatures are bad for battery life: take several spares as well as a charger, and start each shooting session with a freshly charged battery.

8 The nature of the trip means that you'll take many more photos than you can possibly imagine, so take several spare memory cards.

9 Most shots of seals and penguins work better from a low camera angle, but don't kneel or lie on the ground if a seal is within striking or rolling distance*: it's safer to use an articulated viewfinder (one that tilts and swivels) or crouch.

10 Be realistic: sighting a fast-moving whale which blows and surfaces at unexpected intervals and locations is difficult enough. Trying to photograph it may be unduly distracting. Sometimes it's better to put the camera away, live in the moment and enjoy the sighting.

11 If you intend to go sea kayaking or take a polar plunge, you may want to take a small, fully waterproof action camera to record the special occasion, rather than risk your normal camera or smartphone in the cold, salt-water environment. Think about how to keep it accessible but safely captive.

12 Abrupt temperature changes are very bad for cameras: a well-insulated camera bag helps to reduce condensation. Protect your kit by putting it inside a ziplock freezer bag and giving it plenty of time to adjust to the new temperature. A microfibre cloth can help with mopping up snow and protecting the equipment.

* No contact with the ground allowed in season 23/24: see page 2

5 Reference

Further reading

There's a vast library of Antarctic literature. Below is a personal selection of the books that have meant most to me. It may help you to decide which books to seek out or request as presents to read before you leave. In all cases I quote data for the edition that I possess, but many others exist.

First-hand accounts and recreated journeys

South: the Illustrated Story of Shackleton's Last Expedition 1914-1917 Ernest Henry Shackleton QuartoKnows/Voyageur (centenary edition 2019) 978-0-7603-6482-6 381pp

Ghost-written anonymously by Edward Saunders, this book was based on hurried interviews. First published in 1919, it has never been out of print, but it made no money for Shackleton. This version has great photos and facsimile entries from Shackleton's log.

Worst Journey in the World Apsley Cherry-Garrard (originally 1922) Prabhat ebook 362pp

Classic account by a young member of Scott's last expedition who, with Bowers and Wilson, man-hauled sleds to Cape Crozier in July 1911 to collect Emperor penguin eggs in appalling weather – a Force 11 blizzard and -60 °C. George Bernard Shaw encouraged him to write about this 53-day trip, and the fate of Scott and the polar party, and suggested the title.

Home of the Blizzard Douglas Mawson (1996, based on 1930) Wakefield Press 978-1-86254-377-5 438pp

Based on the 1930 'abridged popular edition' of Mawson's two-volume original, this account still provides plenty of detail of the privations and challenges with no trace of drama or self-pity. Well worth tracking down to understand the importance of Mawson's achievements.

Island at the Edge of the World Stephen Venables (1991) Hodder & Stoughton 0-340-55600-5 177pp

This captivating portrait of South Georgia goes beyond an account of an impressive climbing expedition in extreme blizzards. It portrays a fragile island and its amazing wildlife, with great photos and many entertaining incidents on the journey.

Ship beneath the Ice Mensun Bound (2022) Macmillan 978-1-0350-0841-4 395pp

Gripping account of the discovery of the wreck of *Endurance* by a maritime archaeologist who directed the exploration. I was lucky enough to be in Antarctica at the time, which made the book even more exciting.

Mawson: LIfe and Death in Antarctica Tim Jarvis (2008) Miegunyah Press 978-0-522-85486-2 239pp; *Chasing Shackleton* Tim Jarvis (2013) William Morrow/HarperCollins (US edition) 978-0-06-228273-6 264pp; also available as an ebook

These two books provide captivating accounts of how and why Tim Jarvis was moved to recreate two epic journeys by Antarctic heroes Mawson and Shackleton, using authentic clothing and equipment. Both include excellent colour photos that reveal the drama and challenge.

Biographies

Shackleton: By Endurance We Conquer Michael Smith (2015) Oneworld Publications 978-1-78074-707-1 443pp

Carefully researched and very readable, Smith's biography reveals the inner aspects of a complicated personality with huge leadership strengths. He portrays the warmth and charisma of the man, but is honest about his serious failings over the business aspects of his expeditions.

Scott of the Antarctic David Crane (2007) HarperPress 978-0-00-745044-2 637pp

Crane's definitive biography reconciles the extremes of opinion that in the past sometimes lionised and sometimes belittled Scott's leadership. He delves into Scott's childhood and early naval career in a highly readable book with a section of photos.

Wildlife, photography and history

Antarctic Wildlife James Lowen (2011) Princeton University Press (Wildguides) 978-0-691-15033-8 240pp

Outstandingly great field guide to all you are likely to see, helpfully organised and superbly illustrated: highly recommended

A Visitor's Guide to South Georgia Sally Poncet and Kim Crosbie (2005) Princeton University Press (Wildguides) 978-1-903-65708-9 180pp

Spiral-bound guide to the wildlife and vegetation of 24 of South Georgia's popular visitor sites with mapping and photos.

My Penguin Year Lindsay McCrae (2019) Hodder & Stoughton 978-1-529-32545-4 292pp

The author illustrates his account of 11 months filming Emperor penguins for the BBC with great photos. If you've access to BBC iPlayer, you may still catch the one-hour film: *Dynasties* Series 1 programme 2.

Freeze Frame Doug Allen (2012) Tartan Dragon 978-0-9571392-0-6 240pp

Hardback coffee table book with stunning photography of polar regions by an award-winning cameraman and diver who has spent many winters, as well as summers, in Antarctica.

Antarctic Peninsula: a Visitor's Guide (2nd ed 2019) Adrian Fox (editor) Natural History Museum 978-0-565-09465-2 141pp

Scientific approach to climate, geology, oceanography, ice formation, wildlife and politics mediated by the British Antarctic Survey and contributed by eight authors.

Antarctica: a history in 100 objects Jean de Pomereu and Daniella McCahey (2022) Conway 978-1-8448-6621-2 216pp

A great book to dip into, featuring an intriguing collection of objects ranging from Hussey's banjo to Cherry-Garrard's penguin eggs, from a pony snowshoe to the the aurora australis.

Useful websites and sources

We host a selection of over 20 useful Antarctic links here: *bit.ly/RR-AGAlinks*
so that we can maintain and update them online. They include a time-lapse video of the seasonal variation in pack ice, animations of Antarctica's hours of daylight, a webinar in which Tim Jarvis tells the whole story of his recreation of Shackleton's journey, and many more.
We include links to bodies that were important data sources for this book. We thank the British Antarctic Survey (BAS), International Association of Antarctica Tour Operators (IAATO), the Falklands Maritime Heritage Trust (FMHT), Library of the Scientific Committee on Antarctic Research (SCAR), National Snow and Ice Data Centre (NSIDC) at University of Colorado and the Scott Polar Research Institute.

Acknowledgements

We are grateful to many organisations including the BAS, IAATO, NSDIC and SCAR/SPRI (listed above) for their data and for responding to emails. NASA (*nasa.gov*) is the source of most of the aerial photography of Antarctic used in this book.

Various people have kindly helped by commenting on drafts and providing answers to my ceaseless questions. I warmly thank John Anderson, Keir Bloomer, Sheila Cronin, Lindsay and Nicholas Merriman and Lucy Yeoman of Polar Routes. Stephen Venables made many valid points and helped above and beyond the writing of his Foreword. Chiz Dakin's Antarctic experience shone through her comments as well as her excellent photos: see *peakimages.co.uk* for a link to her Photoshelter images. We thank Mark Clydesdale/OpenStreetMap for the maps on pages 20-24.

Photo credits

Chiz Dakin 15, 28, p31, 38 (lower two), 40 (lower), 41 (upper), 42 (main), 51 (and 2-3), 89 (lower), 92; Jacquetta Megarry 18, 24, 27, 39, 40 (upper), 41 (lower two), 43 (both), 45 (both), 64, 77, 80 (upper); Sgt Peter Yokel/*defense.gov* 10 (upper); Oceanwide Expeditions 29; *bit.ly/mvfram* 23; British Antarctic Survey 57, 84; Herbert Ponting (via RGS/SPRI) 60, 68, 69; Franklin Co Eng/Wikipedia 63; Riksarkivet (National Archives of Norway) 66; Frank Hurley 71, 72, 73 (both), 74; Tom L-C/Wikipedia 80 (lower); Paul Larsen/*timjarvis.org* 81; Falklands Maritime Heritage Trust/Endurance 22 82; Andrew Shiva/Wikipedia 85; back cover (Venables) Rodrigo Jordan.

Thanks also to *dreamstime.com* with the following photographers: Steve Gould & Joe Sohm front cover; Nicoelnino title page; Tomas Griger 4-5, 6 (right); Markus Gann 6 (left); Steve Allen 8; Cherylramalho 11, 14 and 90-91, 89 (upper); Vadim Nefedov 12; Frederic Zana 16-17; Mogens Trolle 17 (upper); Martyn Unsworth 19; Jason Row 21; Sharon Jones 26; Martin Schneiter 30; Agami Photo Agency 32, 36 (upper), 37 (upper two), 38 (upper); Serenayuan 33 (upper); Tarpan 33 (lower); Izanbar 34 (upper); Jean Van Der Meulen 36 (upper); Lee Amery 36 (lower); Ndp 37 (lower); Ondřej Prosický 40 (middle); Gentoomultimedia 42 (inset); Staphy 44 (upper), 49; Yitzhak Kohavi 44 (lower); Ken Moore 46 (upper); Steve Bebington 46 (lower); Jeff097 47; Slowmotiongli 48 (upper); Ken Griffiths 48 (lower); Kozzi2 50; Romolo Tavani 51; Serenayuan 54-5; Jan Martin Will 55 (upper); Bernard Breton 56; Patrick Poendl 58-9; Martyn Unsworth 65; Hel080808 86 (both).

Index